Putting the Fun in Fund Raising

Putting the Fun in Fund Raising

Phillip T. Drotning

 Contemporary Books, Inc.
Chicago

Library of Congress Cataloging in Publication Data

Drotning, Phillip T.
How to put the fun in fund raising.

Includes index.
1. Fund raising.   I. Title.
HV41.D76   361.7'3   78-26346
ISBN 0-8092-7627-5

Published by Contemporary Books, Inc.
180 North Michigan Avenue, Chicago, Illinois 60601
Manufactured in the United States of America
Library of Congress Catalog Card Number: 78-26346
International Standard Book Number: 0-8092-7627-5

Published simultaneously in Canada by
Beaverbooks
953 Dillingham Road
Pickering, Ontario L1W 1Z7
Canada

Contents

Introduction

Among the many perceptive observations made by the young Frenchman, Alexis de Tocqueville, when he came to the United States 150 years ago was his description of the laudable proclivity of Americans to band together to solve their own problems and those of others.

"These Americans are a peculiar people," he wrote. "If, in a local community, a citizen becomes aware of a human need that is not being met, he thereupon discusses the situation with his neighbors. Suddenly a committee comes into existence. The committee thereupon begins to operate on behalf of the need and a new community function is established. It is like watching a miracle, because these citizens perform this act without a single reference to any bureaucracy, or any official agency."

If de Tocqueville were to return today he would discover that Americans are even more deeply involved in voluntary, individual acts of charity and concern. A dramatic example was celebrated on Independence Day, 1978, in Shelby, a northern Ohio community of 10,000 people. Two years earlier the residents had decided that Shelby needed a community center. They could have looked to Columbus or Washington for the money, or asked for a bond issue or an increase in property taxes, but instead they chose to demonstrate the independent American spirit that de Tocqueville wrote about. They decided to raise the needed $1.8 million by digging into their own pockets!

More than 2,500 pledges of financial support rolled in. Factory workers asked their employers to have their contributions deducted from their paychecks—an example that prompted their employers to contribute, too. Groups formed to raise funds through carnivals, rummage sales, and auctions. The kids in the community ran car washes.

In just six months they had their $1.8 million!

Shelby opened its recreation center—complete with swimming pool, gymnasium, saunas, adult health facilities, racquetball courts, and meeting rooms—on the Fourth of July. Many of the residents recalled on that day the words of School Counselor Bob Reimsnyder, who two years earlier had helped convince the townspeople that they could do it:

"Towns are playing this government funding game to death," he had said. "America used to be a story of independence and meeting a challenge. It's a story that's been forgotten by too many people."

Shelby, armed with the slogan, "Yes We Can," proved that independence and self-reliance haven't been forgotten there. As businessman Mike Hall said just before the Big Day, "The people of Shelby have done it themselves and they are *so* proud. Everybody's going to be out for the dedication. We're going to have a parade you won't believe. It's going to stretch from downtown all the way to the community center. Little Leaguers, Girl Scouts, Boy Scouts, all the organizations—everybody's going to be in it."

Shelby demonstrated American independence in a more

concentrated setting, but it hasn't been forgotten elsewhere in America, either. It would be difficult to find a family in which at least one member is not involved with some charitable group—the neighborhood church, if nothing else. The magnitude of this involvement is reflected in the numbers: In 1977, of a record $35 billion in charitable contributions in the United States, nearly $30 billion came from individuals and more than half of that from families with incomes under $20,000 a year.

Most of the media attention that philanthropy receives is focused on corporations, private foundations, and individual "heavy hitters" who make substantial contributions that are newsworthy because of their size. Small wonder, then, that most of us are surprised to learn that it is not the most affluent among us who are the primary source of support for charitable enterprises in this country. Instead, individuals who give relatively small sums to their favorite causes, or who exercise their ingenuity and donate their energy to raise large amounts through small donations, surpass the large donors by a margin of six to one.

Even more startling than the dollar amount is the contribution made by millions of individual citizens in the form of personal services. This contribution is valued in excess of $16 billion a year, and represents more than dedication to worthy causes. It also constitutes an enormous investment of blood, sweat, and tears.

Some of this investment in charitable services is made in the form of individual donor solicitation, *e.g.* the mothers across America who annually visit their neighbors in behalf of the March of Dimes. The proceeds from drives of this sort produce a significant portion of the annual budget for most of the major national organizations, particularly those in the health field. The Juvenile Diabetes Association, for example, receives more than half of its funds from individual solicitations made by volunteers who belong to local chapters throughout the 50 states. Huge sums are also produced through a myriad of fund-raising events sponsored by individuals or groups in behalf of charities in their own communities.

One chapter in this book has been devoted to the fine art of begging, and another to the solicitation of major corporations and foundations, but its primary purpose is to assist the millions of dedicated and generous individuals who volunteer to manage or work on local fund-raising events. I've tried to cover every conceivable type of fund raiser, from small to large. You'll find them listed by categories in Section II, so you can pick the ones that suit your fancies, and can be managed successfully by the group with which you work.

I don't promise, when you have reached the last page, that you'll be as successful as Mildred Hurwitz, of Chicago—a volunteer who has personally sold over $20 million worth of Israel bonds. You probably won't even do as well as Mrs. Esther Coopersmith, of Washington, D.C., an unpaid volunteer who is a master of political fund raising. She once served green bagels at an Irish breakfast fund raiser for New York's Senator Patrick Moynihan. Utilizing that kind of ingenuity she has enticed nearly $8 million from reluctant donors.

But then, your own fund-raising goals probably aren't in that league, so you need not be disheartened by the examples. If you are willing to settle for less, the odds are that you can reach your own goals more readily, and even exceed them, if you draw from the experience of thousands of others who have already learned many of the tricks of the fund-raising trade.

After half a lifetime on both sides of the fund-raising street, I wrote this book because I wanted to help others raise money more successfully. I hope it helps you do that. But more important, I hope it will teach you to have fun while you're doing it. It takes a special kind of person to get pleasure from wandering around the neighborhood in the rain, ringing doorbells and importuning neighbors to part with some of their hard-earned cash. How much more satisfying to raise the same money by entertaining those same neighbors at a sensational, fun-filled special event!

The ideas are in the pages that follow, and also the ground rules that spell the difference between success and failure. Study them and you'll raise more than money. You'll raise your spirits, as well!

Phillip T. Drotning
Lake Forest, Illinois

Putting the Fun in Fund Raising

1

What is a successful fund raiser?

The board of directors of the Community Beautification Association is in emergency session. None of the members needs to be told what the emergency is, for disaster is written all over the face of the treasurer as she begins to read her report. The Wolverine Foundation failed to come through with its annual grant, there's a zero balance in the association's bank account, the payroll must be met tomorrow, the local nursery is demanding payment for that last truckload of *Taxus cuspidata,* and not a dollar is in sight.

Richard Replevin, the only lawyer on the board, stirs in his chair, a dour expression on his face, and clears his throat harshly. "You all appreciate, I trust, that we directors can be held personally liable for the obligations of the association!"

All eyes turn to the chairperson, Hortense Honeysuckle, who looms large at the head of the table. "Damn the liability," she snaps, "I'm not concerned about that. I'm worried about Arbor Day. It's only two weeks off and we don't have

1

the money to pay for the plantings we announced for City Hall. We'll all be disgraced! We've simply got to find some money somewhere."

Hortense and her organization are imaginary, of course, but not atypical. The Beautification Association is her creation. She founded it and from the outset has run it as though it were a personal fiefdom. The membership is limited to her own circle of friends, and has grown very little because Hortense wants to maintain the image of a socially exclusive organization. Meanwhile, partly because of the limited membership, the association has developed no real fund-raising capability. It has existed on a few large annual donations made by business associates of the local banker, who happens to be Hortense's husband. Now they have become disillusioned, and the association is in deep trouble.

The situation is not unusual. Many nonprofit organizations have been in similar straits. An unfortunate percentage of voluntary agencies leap from financial crisis to financial crisis, managing nothing better than uncomfortable poverty in between. Those that survive and attain consistent solvency have several things in common with each other, but not with Hortense. For the most part, they are those with the wisdom and energy to identify their long-term financial needs, develop a strong membership base, win community support for their objectives and confidence in their ability, and carefully plan and organize a schedule of fund-raising activities that will enable them to grow and prosper.

It is not that Hortense made a mistake by soliciting funds from substantial donors. No effective organization neglects development efforts aimed at these sources. After all, it is considerably more efficient to raise $10,000 from one donor than it is to solicit $1 each from 10,000 givers. But a realistic board of directors also recognizes that total reliance on a handful of large donors will almost inevitably lead to disaster. Eventually, they will fade away and divert their money to other organizations that offer more exciting goals, or inspire greater confidence. Most major donors don't like to support any organization in perpetuity. They prefer to provide a financial base for a period of time, while the organization develops other sources of financial support; then they want to move on to new projects. Continued reliance on a few major donors, devoid of any effort to develop innovative alternate sources, is of itself a reason for the major donor to cut the organization from his list.

That's why the more successful voluntary organizations rely heavily on neighborhood fund raising, carried out by volunteers among small individual donors, and on special events that are planned and manned by their members. And there's another reason, too. Such events, if they are well-planned, effectively managed, and exciting, are an excellent source of new members for the organization.

How do you measure the success of a fund-raising event? Obviously, the first criterion is money. Was the event profitable? But there are other considerations that are equally important:

Was the event enjoyable for the participants?

It is almost a rule of thumb that the best fund-raising events are those in which the participants come away feeling that they got something for their money. They had fun, were entertained, bought something that they will cherish, enjoyed the satisfaction of helping a worthy endeavor and—don't knock it—on April 15 will be able to deduct from their income taxes at least part of the cost of their pleasure!

An event that fails to meet these standards is a loser even if it makes money, because it has failed to maximize all the values that can be extracted from the occasion. A successful fund-raising event should be so satisfying to the guests that they will want to return next year. It should inspire them to praise the occasion to their friends, expanding the base of potential future customers. Finally, if your guests have a pleasurable, satisfying experience at your fund raiser it will increase their respect for your organization and the cause it espouses.

Did your volunteer workers enjoy the experience?

The success or failure of a benefit event is determined by the dedication, enthusiasm, and energy of the volunteer workers who plan and organize it, and who do the work. It is not enough to plan an event that will be fun for the guests. It must be a happy experience for the workers as well. In fact, if the volunteers are turned off before the event takes place, it will probably be equally disappointing to the guests.

Worker satisfaction depends upon a number of elements. The first, which should be present from the outset in planning an event, is what business calls "participatory management"— which simply means that everyone is included in the planning process. Psychologically, everyone will work harder to make a benefit successful if they have shared in the decision to conduct it. Hortense probably couldn't have expanded her membership, even if she had chosen to do so, because she insisted on dominating the organization and making all the decisions herself.

A second strategy is to allow the workers to choose the tasks that fit their interests and talents. Most people will work at things they enjoy. More important, most of us know our own talents and limitations. It doesn't make much sense to have a crafts-oriented member keeping the books while the math whiz among you is struggling with needlepoint. This process will probably leave some tasks unassigned, but if every member has been given the opportunity to do one thing she likes to do, she won't mind sharing the dirty work with the others.

A third essential to achieve worker satisfaction is to make every stage of planning and organization fun for all of the members. Don't schedule long, boring, unessential meetings; and when you must have one, make it a social event as well. If your event is to be a bazaar, and your members are working on craft projects, don't allow all of their effort to become isolated drudgery. Organize group sessions at which members can work together, catch up on the neighborhood gossip, and perhaps even enjoy coffee and cake or a bottle of wine. If you plan to conduct a rummage sale or an auction, try having some evening events for husbands and wives. The price of admission? A treasure that can be auctioned or sold.

Fourth, share the public credit for the effort that goes into the event. Don't feature the president of your organization or the bazaar chairman in all of the publicity about your event. Look for ways to feature the contributions that are being made by others in the organization. Everyone can't be president or chairman, but most of us like to get credit for the work that we do.

Finally, arrange some special privileges for your members to reward them for their contribution to the event. If you are staging a benefit concert with a "name" entertainer, arrange a pre- or postconcert cocktail party for the star, with your members as guests. If you're conducting a big one-day rummage sale, let your workers shop it the day before. They'll gladly pay ten or twenty percent more than the marked price for the privilege of having first pick. Your organization will get more money for the item, and your workers will have the satisfaction of getting in ahead of the pack.

Did your event expand your membership?

The spark that gets most groups going is mutual concern about a problem, but members are the fuel that keeps your organization alive. The events you schedule should be a major and continuing source of new members. These new members will expand your capacity to schedule ever larger events and will replace members who find other interests or leave the neighborhood.

Obviously, you will attract new members if you demonstrate through your events that yours is a "fun group" to be with.

But remember, different people join organizations for different reasons. Use your events to "sell" the purpose of your organization. Set up a table with membership applications near the door, and staff it with one or more of your most persuasive and knowledgeable members. Invite people to join. You'll be surprised to discover how many of your neighbors would like to belong to your group, but are too embarrassed to solicit an invitation.

Did your event publicize the purpose of your group?

Fund raising is essential to keep your organization afloat, but don't let your preoccupation with financial needs obscure the fact that fund raising is not the purpose of your organization. It is just a means to an end. Incorporate into all of your publicity materials a description of the purposes of your organization and the work that it does. Don't just say that you are conducting a benefit for the Beautification Association. Describe the purpose of the association, and point to some of the important projects that it has completed.

Did your benefit demonstrate your desire to become self-sufficient?

One of the standards by which most major donors judge an organization is the effort that it expends and the success it has had in raising money through its own efforts within the community. In many cities, organizations included in the United Way are judged in part by the amount of community financial support that they have been able to generate.

Major donors are concerned about your community fund-raising efforts because they want the organizations they support to learn to stand on their own feet. But more important than that, they see your fund-raising performance as a quantifiable measure of the enthusiasm of your members and their dedication to the cause that you represent. The major donor wants to feel that his money is benefiting an organization that is effectively managed, and one that is supported by people who are contributing their own money and energy to the cause.

As you develop your fund-raising program, consider whether it will enable you to give positive answers to the questions that have been asked in this chapter. If it does, you probably have an organization that will be able to survive, even in adversity.

2

Organizing for success

In theory, and in the eyes of the Internal Revenue Service (IRS), your group is a nonprofit organization, but that's only because none of your members receive personal financial benefit from any of the funds you collect. In practice your fund-raising events must be for-profit all the way. Your objective is to sponsor fund raisers that will produce income in excess of expenses. The difference, the IRS notwithstanding, is profit that you can use to pursue the objectives of your organization.

When you decide to conduct a fund-raising event, you have decided to go into business. Your success will be determined by most of the same criteria that are used to judge traditional business enterprises, and it will be achieved by applying the same rules and techniques that produce profits for I. Magnin, Warner Brothers, or General Motors.

Your first challenge will be to develop an effective organization. This will not happen by chance, but only as the result of a studied analysis of the work to be done and the structure that will be needed to produce it. You will undoubtedly begin, if only to meet legal requirements, by developing a board of directors and electing a slate of officers: a president, who will bear ultimate responsibility for the operations of the organization; a vice president, who will carry out the president's duties in his absence; a secretary to keep the records that are required for legal and other purposes; and a treasurer, who will be responsible for financial affairs.

Depending upon the objectives of your group, and the kinds of projects that it proposes to undertake, you will also develop a committee structure to deal with the obvious major needs. You will perhaps need a nominating committee, a finance committee, a publicity committee, a membership committee, a research and development committee, and other committees as the need becomes apparent. Since you are working with volunteers who aren't being paid and can't devote full time to the organization, it is wise to break the required effort down into manageable pieces, so that no one committee will be unduly burdened. Inevitably, this will lead to a lot of committees, but so be it. You'll enrich the roles of many of your members, and reduce the possibility that any essential tasks fall between the chairs.

In addition to your basic organizational structure, you will also need to develop separate organizations to manage specific events. If the event is a simple coffee or cocktail party, the organization required will be relatively simple. If it is a major concert benefit, auction, or bazaar, it may be elaborate, indeed. When the Women's Association of the First Presbyterian Church in Lake Forest, Illinois, conducted its 29th annual rummage sale in 1978, the organization included two chairmen, two assistant chairmen, a treasurer, and two administrative committees to handle personnel and publicity. In addition, there were 22 service committees and 28 sales committees, each with a chairman and several members. As the sale day approached, scores of additional workers became involved.

Was it necessary or, more to the point, was it worth it? You be the judge. The rummage sale yielded $49,052.83 for the benefit of more than a dozen charitable endeavors.

Your second organizational requirement, in private enterprise, would be called employee relations. This will be discussed more fully in a later chapter, but there are a number of basics that you must not overlook. They include careful assessment and allocation of available skills, good communications with members, development of devices to build and maintain worker morale, and—where major events are involved—some provision for training new workers based upon the experience gained in prior years.

The third characteristic of an effective organization is prudent management of resources. A major portion of a corporate chief executive's day is devoted to the allocation of physical, financial, and human resources. Your principal asset is people, so you must make certain that their time and energy is used wisely; but capital allocation may also be a requirement. If your organization is large and financially sound, you may be able to increase its assets by investing surplus funds as front money that will allow you to conduct major, highly profitable events. You might, for example, provide the financial guarantees that are required in order to secure a benefit performance by a stage, screen, radio, or television star. Before you do so, though, make a prudent analysis of the risks involved and the potential results to be obtained. If the risk/benefit ratio is acceptable, you can afford to gamble, but not against ridiculous odds.

Effective organizations are never content with current operations. They build in organizational provisions that enable them continuously to increase their efficiency, improve their market penetration, and stay abreast of public needs and desires. Even though you have developed, over the years, one or more successful annual fund-raising events, it is dangerous to rely totally on past successes. Times and attitudes and interests change—and your organization must be prepared to change with them. You must give constant attention, therefore, to product research and market development by providing a place for this function in your organizational structure. Be alert to new interests in your community that could form the basis for a successful fund raiser. Consider innovations that you might introduce to make your traditional events more attractive. It's an axiom that a business changes and grows or it dies. That applies to nonprofit organizations, too.

Other requirements that will influence your success are advertising, publicity, merchandising, and salesmanship. Some of these will be dealt with later, but all of them are crucial, and provision should be made for them in your organizational structure.

But even with all of these organizational resources in place, your organization may not succeed unless you establish firm, measurable goals; timetables for achieving them; and a realistic budget within which the organization will operate. Your budget should reflect the expenditures of the organization for the coming year, geared to the financial resources that you can reasonably expect to be available. Your fund-raising goals must be set at a level that will produce the revenue needed to meet the budgeted objectives. The timetables must ensure that income is available when it is needed, on a predetermined schedule. Many an organization has found itself in trouble because it forgot about cash flow. It doesn't do any good to know that your organization will receive $10,000 in December if it doesn't have the funds with which to pay its bills in June.

Budget preparation should not be passed off as a paper exercise, reflecting the hopes of those who drafted it rather than the realities of your operations. The author was once a director of a statewide social agency in Illinois and protested vehemently year after year when the board approved a budget based on the expectation that more than $150,000 would be received from corporations and foundations. In no one of those years did the actual receipts reach $30,000, so the executive director had to keep rejuggling the budget to stay within the funds available.

Ultimately, when he became president of the association, the author recruited a sharp CPA from one of the Big Eight accounting firms to serve as chairman of the finance committee. By the time he had finished working on the books it was discovered that the association was actually more than $50,000 in the red in its operating accounts. It had been spending grant money earmarked for special projects in order to cover the cost of general operations. It took a year to get the financial mess corrected and the organization back on its feet.

That's why realistic budgets, good accounting, and sound planning are so essential for any organization. You should plan not only for the year at hand, but for the future as well. The successes you have this year should do more than meet immediate needs. They should also build the foundation for even greater progress in the years ahead. They won't if your accounting is so bad you don't know where you stand today, and if you try to operate your organization without looking beyond tomorrow.

Lest you be put off by the demands made on you in this chapter, it should be noted that the complexity of your organizational structure will vary considerably depending on the size of your membership, the thrust of your efforts, and the magnitude of the funds that you require. A women's church group that is organized primarily for religious and social interaction, but has the auxiliary purpose of raising modest sums for charitable purposes, obviously will not require an elaborate organizational structure. But, as your membership increases and the sophistication of your activities develops, your organizational structure must develop apace.

Just be sure that the load you are trying to pull is matched by the horses!

3

How to choose
a suitable event

Your organization has decided to undertake a new project and must increase its budget in order to do it. Several of the members have suggested that you raise the money by sponsoring a benefit, but there is disagreement over what that event should be. How can you resolve the differences, and at the same time make sure that the benefit you select will raise the money that you need?

The success or failure of the event you sponsor will hinge on the care you exercise in determining what it is to be. Too often, in the past, organizations have sponsored fiascos that were selected without careful analysis, simply because other groups had experienced success with similar events. The fact that something has worked well for another group does not mean that it will. work for you. Before you make a decision you need well-researched, honest, and realistic answers to several very important questions:

How much money do you need?

Don't reply, "All we can get!" Placing this question at the top of the list is, in one sense, putting the cart before the horse. But it is important that you ask it if your purpose in conducting a fund raiser is to produce a specific, absolutely essential sum. If your treasury is in a deficit position, and your group can't survive unless it raises $2,000 soon, it would be pointless to sponsor an event that can't possibly raise more than half that amount. Nor would it make any more sense to plan some elaborate benefit that won't produce any returns for several months down the road. You might as well spare your members the effort, because in either case the organization will still be down the tube.

But the other side of that coin is the equally ridiculous decision to sponsor a benefit that has the potential of raising $2,000 when your organization doesn't have the resources to make it work. Several years ago a nonprofit group decided to sponsor a benefit game between the two leading black college football teams. It was to be held in Chicago's cavernous Soldier Field. Although the event had been tried twice and dropped by the city's well-staffed and financed Urban League, the group was convinced that it could do it better. They couldn't, mostly because they overestimated the productivity of the manpower that was available, and it was months before they recovered from the losses they sustained.

Begin your research by determining your financial objective. Then study the potential financial return from a variety of benefit events. If you can't reach your objective by sponsoring a single event that you can manage successfully, consider sponsoring two or three smaller affairs that collectively will produce the same revenue.

What are your human resources?

The one absolutely essential ingredient of a successful fund raiser is people—dedicated, loyal, hardworking, self-sacrificing, cooperative, creative, talented people. Begin your evaluation of human resources by making an honest, realistic appraisal of your members. Don't delude yourself by playing a simple numbers game. Many a benefit, like the one just mentioned, has fallen flat on its face because the chairman made the false assumption that 200 members meant 200 workers. It never does.

In any group of 200 people you'll find some who are indifferent, some who are lazy, some who are irascible, some who are all thumbs, and some who are just plain dumb. Before you can determine how much real help you can count on, you must do an individual appraisal of everyone in the group. Mary Jones always comes through; Jennie Smith never does; Sue Watson is great at crafts; Lucy is a good artist, etc. Pick out the ones you know will work hard, who will be cooperative and uncomplaining, and who have at least one talent that will help the cause. If you are lucky, you will come up with a hard core of workers that probably won't number more than 25 of the 200 in your group. That doesn't mean you won't get some help from the others, but you now know how many you can really count on, and what each of them can contribute.

It is particularly important to assess talent as well as enthusiasm and energy. Do some of your members have exceptional skill in one or more of the crafts? If so, perhaps you should be considering a bazaar. Does your group include semiprofessional artists, actors, or musicians? If the answer is "yes," perhaps you should sponsor an art show or a theatrical performance. Have you one or more members who is a whiz at organization, accounting, or publicity? Is there a real charmer among you who can talk the local merchants out of the things you will need to conduct your event?

Now, look beyond the members themselves at their other personal associations. Whom do they know? Is there one who is a close social friend of a local theater owner who might secure an actor or musician for a benefit performance? Is there another who is a favorite customer of a posh boutique, who might be able to talk the store into helping you sponsor a benefit fashion show? Is one of your members "old society" in your community, with the clout to open some of your town's most exclusive residences to a house tour?

Don't pass over this exercise lightly. Be thorough, because the answers to these questions may be vital in selecting the event that will be most profitable and most enjoyable for your group.

Can you afford to spend money to make money?

If your treasury is empty, you certainly won't be considering a benefit that requires any significant investment up front. But if the financial condition of your organization is sound, and you have a healthy balance in the bank, you may want to consider a major event that requires an initial investment by your group to get it off the ground. You might, for example, sponsor a benefit performance of a Broadway show—which will require that you guarantee part or all of the house—and put up substantial cash in advance.

Events of this kind can be enormously profitable, and require less effort than many others. But they also contain a high degree of risk. You should not get into one unless conservative estimates convince you that it can succeed and that the fiscal health of your organization will not be threatened if you are wrong.

What has your organization tried before?

Unless yours is a new organization, or one that you have been involved with from the beginning, don't neglect to review the history of its fund-raising efforts. What has it tried in the past? What has succeeded and what has failed? Remember the aphorism, "He who ignores history is doomed to repeat it." Don't make the mistake, through ignorance, of repeating past failures or overlooking previous successes, unless you are aware of altered circumstances that make the past experience obsolete.

What has worked in your community?

All communities do not respond in the same way to the same events. What works in one city won't necessarily work in another. A fiddler's contest may be a big deal in Mountain Gap, Kentucky, and a polo match in Oakbrook, Illinois, but no one in his right mind would try to reverse the locations. Study the fund-raising efforts of other organizations in your community. Find out which types worked and which ones didn't. Then pick an event that you know will be appealing to the audience you are trying to reach.

What is the nature of the market?

Communities and neighborhoods differ in many ways: ethnic character, overall affluence, social mores, and countless other distinctions. Before you plan an event, do a careful study of the character of the market. Determine what type of event will have the broadest appeal. That's what a business would do before deciding to enter a community, and that's what you should do, because you have the same objective—to provide potential customers with something that they will want to buy.

The results of your research will help you to decide what kind of an event you should have, where you should hold it, what special features you should offer, and how much you should charge. Determining the price deserves close attention. You don't want to establish prices so high that they turn people away, nor should they be so low that you fail to realize all the profit that the customers will cheerfully provide.

What is the competition?

When you study other organizations to determine what has worked for them, consider also and avoid those events that have already saturated the market in your community. If three of the local churches have well-established and highly success-ful rummage sales, it probably would be a mistake to try to duplicate their success. They have already built a following, established their publicity channels, and very likely are already draining the community of most of its salable second-hand merchandise. Rather than trying to compete with them, probably without much success and alienating the members of three churches in the process, sponsor a different kind of event that their members, too, will enjoy.

Don't overlook timing

You will find many fund-raising events in this book that are seasonal in character. First, of course, are those associated with the most obvious and popular holidays. But beyond specific holiday celebrations are various kinds of merchandise events that are also seasonal. If you plan one of these, don't underes-timate the amount of lead time that is required. For example, if you plan to conduct an ice skate sale about the time the local pond freezes up, don't wait until the fall to begin your work. The best time to begin collecting the merchandise is in early spring, when thoughts have turned to. boating, swim-ming, and tennis, and your neighbors would as soon give your organization their old ice skates as to cart them off to the attic.

What's the "in" thing this year?

We are a nation of fads, and as business entrepreneurs

demonstrate year after year, a potful of money can be made by those who capitalize on them. Observe what's "in" in your community, and determine whether you can build a benefit around it. *Saturday Night Fever* produced a rash of very successful "disco" events all over the country. Use your imagination. Create an "in" event that your group can try— and enjoy.

Do some long-range planning

Any organization can make some money by sponsoring almost any kind of one-shot event. The trick is to maximize the amount of money you raise from the time and effort invested. This suggests the need to select an event that can become an annual affair—a local tradition to which people will want to return again and again. This course of action makes infinitely more sense than a one-shot affair, for many reasons.

First of all, a lot of wasted effort goes into reinventing the wheel. If you sponsor a different type of event each year you will waste a lot of time in the learning process, and never learn to conduct any event at peak efficiency. But if you settle on something that works, and repeat it year after year, your skills will grow, your profits will increase, and you will produce the greatest possible return from the time and energy that your members are able to invest.

You will, of course, make minor modifications in your event as needed to keep it up to date, but the basic mechanics will remain the same. The modifications will probably be limited to additions or changes in exhibits, booths, craft items that are sold. Or, the changes may be strategic. The Arden Shore Association, whose annual benefit fashion luncheon is one of the social events of the season, uses some of its own members as models and for years awarded a single prize to the best model. Ultimately, the producers of the show began having difficulty in persuading models to wear daytime and street attire. Why? Because in previous years, without exception, a model wearing a high fashion evening gown had emerged as best in the show and won the prize. Now prizes are awarded in each of several categories of attire.

Don't underutilize your resources

This chapter has stressed the hazards of undertaking a benefit that is beyond the capacity of your resources, but it is equally inappropriate to underutilize them. The socially conscious individuals who commit their time and energy to your organization, out of a desire to benefit society, deserve to have it well-used. It won't be if your organization is timid or poorly motivated, and repeatedly settles for simple, relatively unproductive projects when it is capable of much more.

The least effective charitable organization is the one that feeds upon itself, limiting participation in its activities to its own members, and thus raising only the funds that are available within the group. Your own members should, of course, contribute generously to their own cause, but their greater value lies in the intelligence and time and energy that they contribute to raise additional funds outside the group.

If you do a conscientious job of analyzing your organization, its needs, its resources, and its opportunities from all of the foregoing perspectives, your group should be prepared to choose intelligently your very own fund-raising event. Once you've done that, you can begin to consider who's going to help you do it.

4

You can't do it alone:
How to recruit
and motivate volunteers

Your ability to organize and conduct your benefit successfully will be determined by the contribution of your members and the others in your community whom they are able to recruit to help. Let's talk about the members first.

Some organizations whose goals are relatively limited and inexpensive to pursue exist on the dues paid by their members. Each member chips in a modest sum each year and this is sufficient to cover the overhead, which may be nothing more than stationery, postage, telephone bills, and possibly a limited amount of local travel expense.

Other groups with more ambitious objectives will require larger budgets, particularly if they reach the point where the activities of the members must be supported by a permanent office location and a paid staff. Your dues structure and membership objectives should be planned to cover as much of this overhead expense as possible, so that the income generated by your benefit events can be devoted to pursuing the

23

basic goals of the organization. The dues your members are asked to pay should not be a matter of random choice. They should be arrived at after careful evaluation of several factors.

First, how much money do you need each year to cover your basic overhead costs? Second, how much can your members afford to pay? If you live in an affluent neighborhood, a higher dues structure will be acceptable than if your members are from middle-class families that are struggling to keep up with inflation. If you have an economic mix within your membership, you may consider two or more levels of dues, such as a higher priced category of "sustaining memberships" for those who can afford it. Finally, what is a prudent estimate of the number of members you can expect to attract in the first year? When you have the answers to those questions, a few simple computations will tell you how much you should ask each member to pay.

Develop a recruiting program

We can assume, if your organization is already in being, that you have established some kind of membership base. This must now become the core of your recruiting organization, assuming that you want to expand your membership as much as possible. Admittedly, organizations differ on this issue. Some thrive by maintaining a closely held membership which endows them with an "exclusive" image. They have a hand-picked hardworking membership which accomplishes with ingenuity, social clout, and energy, what other organizations accomplish with numbers.

There is nothing unacceptable about this mode of operation, but it does have a ceiling on what it can be expected to produce, as compared to a mass membership organization which produces significant revenues in dues, and has the potential of becoming citywide, statewide, or national in scope. If your organization does want to expand its membership, one of the most effective ways is to require that each of your current members accept an annual new membership quota. They should also be required to report periodically on the progress they have made.

Specific individual goals and timetables are, in fact, helpful in the accomplishment of almost everything your organization tries to do. Without them, it is difficult to measure individual performance, and too many of your members will simply let things slide. It's not that they are lazy or unconcerned but that each of us has many priorities in life, and we are inclined to deal with those that are making the most insistent demands.

So, you have your basic core of members, and each of them has accepted the obligation to recruit a specific number of new members during the year ahead. They know that they will be required to report periodically on their progress, and that their peers will be looking over their shoulders to see how well they perform. What can the organization do to make it easier for them to attract their quota of new members?

In this context, you should think of your members as salespeople, because their job is to *sell* the organization to prospective members. It is up to the leadership of your group to give them something to sell! Just as successful businesses advertise and publicize their products and services in order to win customers, so must you *do a good job of publicizing the goals of your group,* and your achievements, in ways that make them appear worthy and attractive. Don't become obsessed with the notion that yours is the only game in town. All of us have a broad range of choices in determining the charitable objectives and social action that we want to pursue. You must convince prospective members that your objectives are significant, your organization is solid, and your members the kind they would like to be associated with.

It is essential that you operate an efficient, effective organization. You need to do this anyway, in order to achieve your basic objectives, but it is also important to your recruiting efforts. Build a record of accomplishment, and publicize your victories. Everyone prefers to ride a winner, so if you do a good job and make sure that people know about it, you won't have to look for new members. They'll be coming to you!

Earn a reputation as a fun organization. Charitable endeavors don't have to be dull. People should see your group as one that does good work and enjoys doing it.

Do everything you can to develop a prestigious image. Try to be the "in" group that everyone in the community would like to be part of. This doesn't mean that you have to be snobbish or unjustifiably restrictive in your membership. It does mean that you do everything you can to earn a reputation as the group that is doing the important things in the community, involves the important people, and endows its members with credit for associating with good people, having fun, and getting things done.

Be democratic, polite, and considerate. Every group must have an organizational structure to keep things moving. It must have a leadership group to make policy decisions, officers to make administrative decisions, and rules and regulations to keep things running smoothly. But it is well for those directors and officers to remember that you can't successfully run a voluntary organization for very long with dictatorial methods that might be acceptable in a business organization. Your volunteers must be made to feel that they have a voice in the decision-making process, that the leadership respects them, and that their contributions are valued. It is especially important to bring new members into the action quickly, so that they will have a good feeling about the group. Don't forget, you want them to start recruiting new members, too, and if they have had a bad initial experience themselves, they aren't apt to enlist others.

Don't let a new member flounder for several meetings trying to get acquainted and having nothing specific to do. Before the first two or three meetings, a member of your group should be assigned to telephone the new member, offering a ride to the meeting. It's more comfortable to arrive at a meeting with another member who knows her way around.

Once the new member is there, make sure that she meets everyone and after that is not ignored. Some groups have found that they can increase attendance and win the loyalty of younger members by providing a babysitting service for those with young children.

Give all your members something specific to do. Then they will feel wanted, needed, and be convinced that their participation is worthwhile. You want them to talk about the importance of what they're doing to their friends, who are prospective members, too.

Look outside your organization

When you are sure that you have your members fully committed and involved, it is time to explore the volunteer resources that are available outside your organization. The best way to begin is by assessing your needs, determining which of them can be met within your own membership, and then exploring how the others may be obtained from outside sources.

Let's begin with manpower needs. Is your group affiliated with a church? If so, what resources are available among the general membership? Does your organization support a residential institution—a boys' or girls' school or senior citizen facility, for example? If so, what help can you get from the residents?

What about other groups in the community that are not essentially charitable in purpose? Can you persuade the Boy Scouts or Girl Scouts to take on some aspect of your event as a community service project? What about the Rotary Club or the Junior Chamber of Commerce? Can they be persuaded to provide some volunteers?

Don't overlook senior citizens. There are undoubtedly many retired men and women in your community who have a variety of highly developed skills which they would cheerfully contribute to a worthy project—if they were asked. Are you having a bazaar? Perhaps you can secure help from elderly residents of nursing homes who are skilled at various crafts, and would gladly make things for you if you will supply the materials they need.

An always productive procedure is to brainstorm with your own members about who might be willing to make some kind of contribution to your event. Do they have friends with specific skills who, for one reason or another, don't want to make a long-term commitment as members of an organization, but would be pleased to contribute their talents on a short-term basis to a specific event? Many organizations have found it effective to conduct a luncheon to which members can bring special guests to expose them to the purposes of the group, outline its needs, and invite them to help or join the group.

Do any of your members have friends with unusual skills that might form the basis of a fund-raising event? An auctioneer, perhaps, who would donate his services to conduct an auction in your behalf. A popular radio announcer who will swell the crowd at a luncheon or dinner by agreeing to serve as master of ceremonies. A theater owner who may be able to entice a famous actor or musician to donate his services for a benefit performance in your organization's behalf.

Does one of your members know a merchant who, for the publicity, will provide what you need for a special event for your own members or for the public at large. A wine-tasting or wine and cheese party, for example. Are several of your members such good customers of a posh local dress shop that they can persuade the owner to put on a fashion show?

Do you have a member who is a really aggressive shopper? Someone who has the courage and salesmanship to persuade local merchants to sell you what you need at a discount, or even let you have it free?

Don't overlook the spouses

Don't forget that most of your members, in addition to

friends and acquaintances, have spouses, too. Can one of the husbands get your printing done without cost at his office? Does another have access to a Xerox machine? Are others professionals who can provide legal, public relations, or accounting services? Is one a potential source of surplus furniture or office equipment? Can others supply merchandise that can be sold at auction? Does one have access to a company auditorium or dining facility that you can use to conduct an event? Can another induce his advertising agency to help obtain entertainment for a benefit, and help promote it, too?

Some organizations have discovered that the best way to find the answers to these questions is to conduct periodic functions for husbands and wives. There the president or chairman frankly discusses the organization's critical needs, and asks whether any of the husbands or wives can help. It may be a little sneaky, but it is not a bad idea to arrange in advance for one of the spouses present to respond immediately with an offer of help on one of the items. That puts the others on the spot—challenges their ego—and they feel compelled to volunteer something, also.

The point is to identify and exploit every conceivable source of support within and outside your organization. That is not as difficult as it seems, if you carefully analyze your essential needs, and then consider all of the more sophisticated refinements you might add to enhance the appeal of the event, add to the pleasure of those who attend, and promote it as widely as possible.

With your volunteers in place, you must now consider how to motivate them to maximum effort, and how to use their time and talents wisely. A list of volunteers is worthless if each individual remains uninspired to do any real work. You must consider time and energy your principal asset and make certain that both are used effectively and efficiently.

Although you want to give your volunteers an opportunity to determine what their contribution will be, you will soon find that a little tactful guidance is in order. Some of your members may have an exaggerated notion of their skills or productivity. Don't let them volunteer for tasks they can't do well, or for more work than you know they can handle.

Break the project down into sufficient individual functions so that every member can find something to do. Then by mutual agreement of the membership, require that everyone contribute a specific number of hours to the project. Require that those who fail to contribute their time and effort compensate the organization by making a monetary contribution to the event. But remember, the object of the penalty is to encourage them to work, so don't set an amount so small that it will allow a member to cop out cheaply.

Put as many of your members as possible in charge of something. It will increase their sense of participation, and their commitment, because they know that they will be singled out as personally responsible if their piece of the effort fails.

Be realistic about your expectations. If you demand too much of your members, you may turn them off; but if you expect too little, they may interpret that as a lack of confidence, and be turned off, too.

Rotate assignments from year to year to avoid boredom, introduce new ideas to the task, and prevent individuals from preempting the choice assignments. If, for example, you conduct an annual fashion show, don't let one group of members repeatedly serve as models. After all, they should take their turn at being wardrobe mistresses, table decorators, or ticket sellers.

Don't rely so heavily on any one member that her failure could jeopardize the success of the event. The engineers built a lot of redundancy into the Apollo spaceship that went to the moon, and you should incorporate backup provisions in your organization, too.

Keep track of progress

Systematically   monitor   the   progress   of   each   of   your members. They'll be flattered that you consider their role to be important, and you will be spared the discovery, the day before the event, that some of your members have dropped the ball. If you conclude that one of your members simply isn't going to deliver what is expected of him, tactfully suggest that he/she may have been given more to do than was reasonable, and offer to find someone who will help. If he declines the help, the odds are he'll feel more obligated to do the work. If he accepts it you will have put things back on the track, and the work will be done by somebody else.

Send out postcards to remind people of deadlines. They're often more effective than a phone call, which is easily forgotten. A postal reminder on the bulletin board hangs there nagging at you. It doesn't go away.

Publish a simple directory that lists in detail all of your committees, and lets everyone in the organization know who's responsible for what. Your members will enjoy the recognition, and the directory will be a helpful aid to communications within the organization.

Publish a timetable that recites completion dates for each element of your preparations. Issue periodic reports to the membership on the progress that has been made. You'll find that the members who are behind schedule will be motivated to catch up so that they're on target when the next report is issued.

Consider awarding prizes or giving some other form of recognition to members who excel in various areas of activity. A competitive spirit among members is always a motivating force.

Finally, don't save your thanks and praise until after the event. Your members will work more diligently if they are praised and encouraged and reassured as the preparations proceed. Remember, you're asking your volunteers to work in what is essentially a business enterprise, without the financial rewards that are derived from other types of work. Their only reward is a sense of achievement and personal satisfaction, and you should make certain that they receive it in large measure.

5

Producing a winner through effective promotion

W hy do some superb motion pictures disappear from the theaters in a few days, while others of lesser quality run almost forever and earn tens of millions of dollars? Why do ordinary and even inferior novels ride the crest of the best seller lists for months while countless others of superior literary quality fail to find shelf space in the local bookstore?

The answer, in most cases, is adroit merchandising, promotion, and publicity. We live in a promotional age—one in which public wants and needs are *created* and most products are sold by applying sophisticated advertising, merchandising, and public relation techniques. Although you are planning a nonprofit function for charitable purposes you must, nonetheless, compete for public attention with commercial enterprises that have enormous promotional resources at their disposal. Without an effective promotion and publicity program of your own you can't expect to produce maximum revenue from your event.

Select an effective publicity chairman

One of the most important choices you will make is the selection of your publicity chairman. You must identify a member with the time, energy, and enthusiasm to study the art of publicity and promotion and apply this knowledge with imagination, diligence, and skill. Too many events fall short of their potential because this vital function is entrusted to a chairman who sees glamor in the job but lacks the creativity and dedication to do it well. Inevitably, the result is one or two ineptly written press releases, submitted without regard to deadlines so that they get minimum space and poor position if, in fact, they see print at all.

In relationships with the media your publicity chairperson should be honest and candid, polite, helpful, and accessible. This person should be able to write clearly, have some knowledge of the media, or at least be willing to learn. The publicity chairman's ego should be second to the interests of the group. The objective is to get publicity for the organization, not for its publicist. Your chairman should also be a well-organized person who is capable of planning and executing an effective publicity program that will be maintained throughout the year. Finally, if the person chosen is a capable typist, it will help.

The first objective of your publicity program will be to develop a solid reputation for your group as one that is engaged in an important and worthy cause which it is pursuing with diligence and skill. You want to develop the public image of an organization that your media audience will want to support and even join.

The second objective is the more specific task of selling each event that your organization sponsors. You want to make your event sound appealing and attractive and come across as a fun occasion that everyone in the community will want to be a part of. How will your chairman achieve this objective?

The press

The most obvious vehicles for publicizing your event are, of course, the newspapers in your community. But knowing the obvious won't take you very far if your publicity chairman has failed to learn the basics of newspaper publicity. Admittedly, most editors will make some allowances for volunteer publicists that they would not make for paid professionals, but you are also competing for space with those paid professionals, so it is important to do the job well.

Here are some of the requirements: Knowledge of the media is basic to an effective publicity effort. You should become thoroughly familiar with the operations of the local press, radio, and television stations. This includes awareness of special sections that carry information about charitable events, calendars of events that include such functions, columnists who will include interesting or humorous items that also mention your organization or event, and weekly newspapers that offer free advertising space to charitable organizations.

It is important to learn, if you haven't already, the mechanics of preparing an effective and publishable press release or spot announcement for the electronic media. A good newspaper article is written in clear, simple, concise language. It presents, preferably in the first paragraph, the "who, what, when, where, and why" of the story. Succeeding paragraphs will elaborate on this information, explain the goals of your organization, and feature the names of individuals who are contributing significantly to the event. If the event requires the advance purchase of tickets, don't fail to state clearly where and how they may be obtained and what they cost.

The press release should be long enough to get your message across, but not so tedious that it repels the editor. Study the media that will receive your material and design your press releases to fit the style and length that they normally accord to functions like yours. At the top of the first page indicate a release date, which usually will be "For Immediate Release," unless there is some special need to delay publication. Also provide the name and telephone number of a publicity contact person who will be available and able to answer questions.

Familiarize yourself with the deadlines of all the media you expect to use. Most newspapers have firm deadlines for each issue, beyond which they will not accept announcements for benefit events. Frequently, the deadline may be two weeks or more prior to the publication date. Newspapers have to handle last-minute spot news in a hurry. When they are up against their publication deadline, they understandably don't want to be bothered with announcements that could and should have been submitted well in advance. A handwritten press release is the last thing a harried city editor wants to see when he is racing against time to get the next edition out.

If you submit your material well in advance of the deadline you will increase the chances of its being published and given a good position. The editor has the opportunity to handle it at leisure and it may well be in type when late material arrives.

Supply good photographs to illustrate your story. Many newspapers will print a photo if it is sharp and clear and the subject matter is fresh and appealing. Don't waste your film on a group photo of your committee chairpersons, or a picture of a donor presenting a check to your president. Rarely will they be used, and even if they are they won't be of interest to anyone but those who are pictured and their family and friends. Use your imagination and develop action shots of people doing interesting, exciting, or novel things. Your purpose, remember, is to get the editor to print the photo, and his subscribers to read what is printed beneath it.

Get acquainted with media people

Without making a nuisance of yourself, begin systematically

to get acquainted with the newspaper, radio and television reporters and editors that can be most helpful to your cause. You'll learn what they are looking for, how they like to have material presented, and what their pets and prejudices are. The person responsible for a section featuring charitable events receives a stack of press releases in every mail. Choices are made as to which will be used and how extensively they will be featured. If you have made a good impression on the editor it is more than likely that your release will receive preference over one submitted by a stranger. That's not favoritism, it's just human nature.

Don't content yourself with the obvious departments. A short item in a popular gossip column can be worth more to you than ten inches in the main news section. Try to become known to the local columnists by supplying them with ideas, not necessarily related to your own organization. Filling a newspaper column five days a week is a demanding chore, and columnists are grateful for bright, interesting, publishable items. If you have sparked the interest and earned the gratitude of a columnist by repeatedly supplying him with items he could use, he will be more receptive when you send him others that relate to your own organization. Quid pro quo, you know.

Develop a planned schedule of newsworthy happenings that will occur periodically during the weeks preceding your event. No editor will respond positively to a stream of press releases which simply restate in different words the basic information about the event you have scheduled. He *will* mention it as part of a story about another newsworthy activity. The women of the Lake Forest Presbyterian Church helped raise their $50,000 by planning a series of preliminary events that served a useful purpose and generated publicity as well.

Finally, don't overlook newspaper advertising possibilities. Many organizations solicit merchandise for auctions and rummage sales by inserting small ads in neighborhood or suburban weekly newspapers. If your event is a big one, such as a theatrical benefit performance, an investment in advertising may be essential to fill the house. But before you decide to spend the money, determine whether there are ways in which you can obtain the space "for free." Some merchants will include a small box in their regular advertisements calling attention to your event. Others may agree to sponsor an ad devoted entirely to your event, receiving a credit line at the bottom that acknowledges their contribution. And in some cities there are advertising councils, formed as joint ventures of the media and the advertising agencies, to provide public service space for nonprofit organizations.

Radio and television

Because they are allocated a monopoly on a piece of the airwaves, radio and television stations are required by the Federal Communications Commission to devote a portion of their programming to public service programs or messages. They must report, as part of their application for license renewal, the extent to which they have fulfilled this obligation.

You can capitalize on this requirement by making information about your organization and its activities known to the public affairs directors of your local television and radio stations. Many stations broadcast daily calendars of events. Others will carry separate spot announcements of the more significant benefit events in the community. Visit the studios and meet the personnel responsible for this programming to determine what their interests, ground rules, and deadlines are. Some television stations will accept short videotape announcements if they are well-executed. In recent years videotape production equipment has become more accessible. One of your members may be employed by a firm that has this equipment and will produce your announcement for you, or have it produced by its advertising agency. Equipment may also be available at one of your local schools. In that case, try to find a producer—perhaps from one of the local advertising agencies—who will donate his services to help you produce an effective and usable tape.

Other publicity outlets on both radio and television are the interview and panel type shows, usually broadcast during daytime hours, which have a broad audience among the homemakers in your community. The producers of these shows are constantly searching for interesting and appealing guests and subject matter. If you present a convincing case for your organization, suggest an imaginative theme for a discussion of its activities that will have broad audience appeal, and then offer an interesting or noteworthy personality from your group who can appear on the program, you may be able to get on one or more of these shows.

Finally, don't overlook the disc jockeys and talk shows. They often will mention charitable events on their programs, particularly if you can provide them with a humorous or emotional framework in which to present it. In some cases they can be encouraged to feature an event, if it involves athletics or entertainment, by supplying them with a block of tickets which they can offer to their listeners for use by underprivileged children, the handicapped, or senior citizens in the community. You can also arrange with the producers of the talk shows that accept telephone calls from listeners to have one of your members call in and present information about your benefit. Again, however, you should be able to offer some clever or amusing gimmick to give the excuse for talking about your event.

The potential of the more popular talk shows is enormous. In Chicago, during the pre-Christmas season each year, a Needy Children's Fund is collected for the purchase of gifts for children selected by the Cook County Welfare Department and the Illinois Department of Public Aid. The idea for the fund came originally from Norman Ross, a popular local radio personality who is also a vice-president of the First National Bank of Chicago. Ross promotes the fund on his own radio show, and funds are collected by the *Chicago*

Tribune and the *Chicago Sun-Times*, but the star performer is Wally Phillips, the city's most popular talk show host. In 1977, the fund raised a total of $1,555,962.03. Of that total, $1,002,847.63 came from listeners who responded to the creative and persuasive appeals of Wally Phillips!

Signs, posters, billboards

Most neighborhood merchants, if asked to do so by a good customer, will post signs advertising your event in their windows or elsewhere in the store. You can get a little extra mileage from the posters by conducting a contest—among the local Girl Scouts, for example—and awarding prizes for the best posters. It is the responsibility of the juvenile artist not only to draw the poster, but to find a store that will display it. Your event benefits from the posters and also from the publicity about the contest itself. It is important that you study your community to determine the locations with high density pedestrian traffic—the local commuter railroad station, for example—and arrange to place signs there.

Canvass the supermarkets in your area and determine which ones maintain bulletin boards on which announcements can be posted. Many stores provide this service for customers who have things to sell, want odd jobs, or are looking for babysitters. Large numbers of shoppers peruse them daily, and your announcement, if it is there, will get attention. Also determine whether there are local businesses that maintain electrified expressway signs available to charitable organizations to flash messages about their events. Check to determine whether you can place an announcement on the marquee of an abandoned movie theater, or on the entrance signs of local motels. Talk to the public relations people of your local billboard companies. Often they will donate space on billboards that are not currently in use. Bus and subway car cards offer a similar opportunity.

But don't make the mistake of putting up your signs and posters too far in advance of your event. You want maximum impact during the two or three weeks immediately before it takes place. If you put them up too early they may already have disappeared by the time that critical period arrives.

Ask for help from other organizations

The resources of other nonprofit organizations in your community can also be exploited to publicize your event. Ask the program chairmen of the local service clubs and other social organizations to include an announcement of your benefit at one of their regular meetings. Determine which groups, including the local churches, publish weekly or monthly newsletters for their members. Ask them to include an announcement in the issue that immediately precedes your event.

Be creative; try to develop some stunts that will attract attention to your event. Consider a street parade with a sound truck, contests that will attract attention, and any other device that will make people aware of your event.

If you are conducting an auction, rummage sale, or raffle, use some of the merchandise as display material to lure people to the event. In some communities, local merchants will make window space available for the display of antiques or other items that will be sold or auctioned by your group. If you have a major prize in a raffle, try to display it in a bank lobby or other high traffic area. If the prize is an automobile, obtain permission to park it in a shopping center parking lot, or other high traffic public location. It will call attention to your event, and you can also increase the profits by setting up a table and selling tickets on the spot.

Put your own members to work

Your members should be encouraged to conduct a perpetual word-of-mouth campaign calling attention to your benefit. But you can also give them more specific tasks to perform. Organize a telephone campaign to inform people of your benefit, and ask the help of your members to address envelopes for a direct mail campaign. But remember, these are time consuming and costly promotional devices, so you should develop your lists with great care. Ask your members to determine whether the companies they or their spouses are associated with have mailing lists of people who would be interested in an affair such as yours. See if you can borrow lists from other organizations. Ask your members to develop their own lists of friends, neighbors, relatives, and business associates. Personalized efforts such as these are among the most effective you can use. It is one thing to read about an event in the newspaper, but quite another to be invited to attend it by a friend.

The importance of planning

As with every other aspect of your organization's efforts, planning is essential if you are to develop an effective publicity program. You should plot your publicity activities carefully, and pay particular attention to timing. You want to exact from the press and other media the maximum amount of coverage possible, but you must also avoid deluging them with repetitious copy and wearing out your welcome.

Finally, your publicity effort should begin modestly and build in intensity as the day of your event approaches. It does a politician no good to be the most popular candidate six months before the election, and a bum on election day. It does your organization no good to have the public intensely aware of your bazaar or auction or garage sale six months in advance and be allowed to forget it as the day of the event approaches. You want to have a concentrated publicity effort, with all the forces coming into play in the final week before the day of reckoning.

Promotion is the single most important element of any effort that requires public participation. Do it well and your event can't miss!

6

Managing the money

The future of your organization and the success of its efforts depend upon your ability to raise money, but many groups have succeeded at fund raising and subsequently collapsed because they didn't know how to manage the money they raised. The complexities of financial management will differ greatly, of course, depending on the size, nature and purpose of the organization concerned. But no organization can afford sloppy accounting practices that prevent it from knowing, at any moment, exactly where it stands.

A great deal of money is raised for charity in America by small, closely knit groups that were organized primarily for social purposes. Their principal activity is organizing social occasions for the entertainment of their members, but out of genuine social concern they have decided to use these affairs to generate financial support for one or more worthy charities. Because the primary source of funds is the members them-selves, everyone can count noses and know about how much a dinner or a dance produced. Obviously, for a group such as this, only a simple set of accounts is needed.

If, however, your organization is or expects to become more than a small neighborhood social club, wants to expand its membership, sponsor major fund-raising events, and raise substantial sums for the cause you espouse, one of your first acts should be to put your legal and financial house in order.

Your first step should be to establish the legal basis of your organization. This will probably require, depending on where you live, that you incorporate as a nonprofit charitable enterprise, registered with the secretary of state or some other state government entity. In some cities you may also be required to obtain a municipal permit or license to operate. In some cities, too, credibility will require that you register and secure the blessing of the Better Business Bureau, the local Association of Commerce, or any other group that maintains a roster of accredited charitable organizations.

Obtaining an IRS tax exemption

Most of these agencies, in ensuing years, will require that you submit annual financial statements, so a good accounting system is an absolute necessity. Further, if you intend to solicit foundations, corporations, and other large donors, it is essential that you obtain certification as a tax-exempt organization under section 501(c)3 of the Internal Revenue Code. Many foundations have charters that permit them to give only to organizations that have such status. If you fail to secure it you will cut your organization off from many sources of substantial financial support.

When you apply for a grant, most foundations will ask you to supply a copy of the "tax determination letter" that is issued by the IRS to declare your tax-exempt status. Obtaining one can be a lengthy process, so don't delay filing your application. If you file before your group has been in operation for eight months you will receive an advance ruling from the IRS which grants a temporary tax-exempt status for a period of two years. At the end of that time you will have 90 days in which to file for permanent status. If you don't, you will lose your exemption.

You will probably need the assistance of an attorney to prepare your application to the IRS (hopefully, you'll have one on your board!). However, documents are available from the Superintendent of Documents, U.S. Government Printing Office, Washington, D.C. 20402, which will provide the information that you need to prepare an application, as well as other tax information of value to nonprofit groups. Ask for Publication 557, *How to Apply for Recognition of Exemption for an Organization,* published by the IRS. It is a 20-page pamphlet that costs 45 cents. It will tell you what application forms to secure from the Internal Revenue Service.

While you're at it you might as well order Publication 561, *Valuation of Donated Property* (35 cents), which explains how to determine the taxable value of donations of merchandise and other gifts other than cash; and Publication 526, *Income Tax Deductions for Contributions* (35 cents), which explains what types of charitable deductions can be claimed, and the organizations that are eligible to receive them.

Restrictions on 501(c)3 organizations

Be forewarned that when you obtain 501(c)3 status in order to become eligible for foundation grants, you become subject to limitations on your activities that were imposed by the Tax Reform Act of 1969. Foundations may not make grants to organizations that:

1. *Seek to influence legislation by lobbying or publicity.* It is permissible to respond to legislative requests for information, but not to *initiate* contact with legislators or with the public regarding partisan legislative issues.

2. *Seek to influence elections or voter registration drives.* There are some exceptions to this prohibition involving

broadly based nonpartisan studies and voter registration drives that are carried out while adhering to strict governmental regulations.

3. *Provide support to an individual for study, travel, or similar purposes* unless such financial assistance has been awarded objectively and without discrimination, following procedures approved in advance by the IRS.

4. *Support an activity that would normally not be tax deductible.* This, in effect, restricts your activities to purposes commonly accepted as religious, charitable, or educational.

If your annual gross receipts exceed $5,000 you will be required to file IRS Form 990 within five months of the end of your fiscal year. This makes it imperative that you keep complete and accurate financial records and develop a good accounting and auditing system. Depending upon the complexity of your accounts and the magnitude of your cash flow, you may also need to submit your books to an annual audit by an independent outside accounting firm. Some major donors will demand such an audit before they will consider your application for financial support.

If you employ any people, or sell any taxable merchandise, you will also need good records so that you can file accurate reports and pay taxes on a timely basis. You may have to pay social security and federal unemployment taxes, and also withhold federal and state income taxes from the wages you pay your employees. State and local sales tax payments may also be required for some activities.

Make certain from the outset that you know precisely what your tax obligations are. Explore whether you can make any changes in your stated purpose that will qualify your group for additional tax exemptions. And never, never fail to pay your tax obligations in full and on time. Some nonprofit organizations have been put out of business because they failed to meet promptly their obligations to the IRS. It's easy to fall into that trap. Withheld employee income taxes, for example, must be remitted to Uncle Sam on a quarterly basis. These funds should be set aside in a separate account at the end of each payroll period. Some organizations, instead of doing that, have succumbed to the temptation to "grease the wheel that squeaks." Short on cash, and under pressure from creditors, they have used their cash flow to pay other bills without reserving the amount required to meet their withholding tax obligations. At the end of the calendar quarter, when the taxes were due, they found themselves without the funds needed to pay them. The same process then continued into the next quarter, and the next, until finally the IRS clamped down. At that point they were in trouble with the most uncompromising creditor there is. The IRS will not forgive your debt simply because you are impelled by charitable motives.

The importance of planning

Good financial records are also important because they are the basis for most of your short- and long-range planning. You can't develop a realistic budget for the next year if you don't know where you will stand at the end of this one. You need complete records of contributions as the basis for future solicitations and in order to realistically estimate your probable income for the following year. A group whose treasurer keeps the records on the backs of old envelopes may find itself with a lot of old envelopes and no money in the bank.

Good accounts and periodic audits are also necessary to reassure prospective donors and to guard the organization against fraud. We would all like to believe that everyone in our group is honest, but more than one nonprofit organization has had a treasurer who disappeared with all the money it had collected so laboriously. Good records, and financial reports reviewed regularly by the membership, will sound warnings of potential financial trouble, reveal areas where spending is excessive and others where receipts are behind expectations, pinpoint incompetence, and expose dishonesty.

If possible, try to recruit a top-notch CPA to head your finance committee and serve on your board. Ask him to work with your treasurer to set up an adequate and foolproof accounting system. Maintain overall financial records, but also do a separate accounting for each fund-raising event you sponsor. You need to know which of your activities are financial winners and which ones lose money, or require more effort than the financial results are worth.

Be sure that your bookkeeping system makes it possible for you to monitor your discretionary expenditures carefully. Is the telephone bill getting out of hand? Are you spending too much for postage or travel? Maybe some tighter controls are necessary. Remember, outgo as well as income determines your bottom line.

Invest surplus funds and avoid borrowing

If you have surplus funds, look for advice on how to invest them wisely. Don't maintain excessive balances in noninterest-bearing checking accounts, and limit the amounts that you carry in ordinary savings accounts. The interest rates on these accounts won't keep up with inflation at current rates, so the money you keep in them will decrease in value every year, even though it increases in actual amount. Look for other investments that will keep ahead of inflation, because their increases in value tend to keep pace with the decline in the value of the dollar.

If you do cautious financial planning and gear your activities and your budget to your available cash and your "certain" income, you should be able to avoid having to borrow to meet your obligations. Nevertheless, even prudent organizations encounter unexpected financial problems. A grant that was promised doesn't come through. An ad book that has always generated $2,000 produces only half that sum—and suddenly you are in financial trouble.

If your group has a solid history, a reputable board of directors, and an excellent credit record, you probably will be able to stave off your creditors by telling them what your problem is and how and when you expect to meet your obligations. Identify a specific source of future income that you will use to pay their bills. Tell them precisely when you intend to pay. In all probability they will go along with you, but if not you may have to borrow. In that event, do some research and shop for the best deal you can make. Interest rates vary and you should try to find the lowest rate you can get. You will be in the best position to deal with this and other financial matters if, early on, you have found an experienced, professional financial advisor who is sympathetic to your cause and will donate advice and counsel when you need it.

Always remember, though, that if you burden your organization with debt you also limit its ability to launch new efforts in behalf of the cause you espouse. You must raise the money to pay your debts before you can begin to use your income for other projects. You will also waste a portion of your receipts in order to pay the interest. That's why prudent nonprofit organizations avoid unsecured debt unless there is no alternative.

That doesn't apply, of course, if you decide to go into debt to buy your own building so you can stop paying rent, or if the purpose of your activity is to build a facility for community use, or to construct housing for low income families. In cases like these you may have to borrow in order to carry out your purposes, but the difference is that the loans are secured by property with value in excess of the amount of the debt. They can be retired by the sale of the property if that becomes necessary.

Another area I won't dwell on, but which should concern

you, is that of insurance coverage. You may want to provide insurance benefit plans for your employees, if you have any. You should protect your organization from liability for unavoidable accidents to those who attend your benefit events. You may even want to protect your directors by insuring them against expenditure responsibility or other liability arising from their involvement with your group. These are all highly specialized forms of insurance which you should explore with a competent insurance broker.

Exercise firm cash control

A final word about money: Pay close attention to the handling of cash receipts from your special events. You may assume that all of your workers are honest, but it is prudent to make sure that none of them is tempted to prove you wrong. The safest procedure for handling cash is one in which at least two people are involved in every transaction. If you are running a cash bar, have one person sell drink tickets and another collect them. If you sponsor an auction, have a bookkeeper prepare a duplicate list of bids as they are received. One copy will go to the cashier who collects the money. The other can be used to check the total receipts when the event is over.

If you sponsor a carnival put on by one of the traveling carnival groups, and are entitled to a share of the receipts, use a ticket system for payment at all the rides and concessions. Members of your organization sell the tickets from numbered rolls (which it supplies) and the carnival operator is reimbursed only for those he returns. This ensures that you will get your percentage of all the cash collected, and perhaps a little more because there will be some customers who still have unused tickets when the event is over.

Cautious cash control—I'd say "foolproof," but there is no such animal—will ensure that your organization actually receives all of the money that is taken in at an event. I know of one situation—an annual carnival conducted by the members of a volunteer fire department—where for years the cash was collected by the workers who manned the concessions. The carnival grossed a relatively consistent $40,000 a year. Finally, a new chairman took over and installed a ticket system. The carnival that year attracted the usual number of participants, but the gross receipts suddenly leaped to almost $55,000!

7

Getting ready for next year

The party's over. You've issued a press release dramatizing the results of your benefit, pointing out the constructive uses to which the money will be put, and thanking the community for its support. You have arranged for proper storage of materials, displays, equipment, signs, and other items that can be reused next year. The donated facility in which you held your benefit is empty and you left it cleaner than you found it. What do you do next?

If your fund raiser is an annual event, or you plan to make it one, the time to begin preparations for the future is the moment when you have finished cleaning up after the event that just ended. No matter how successful your recent experience, you should regard your event as a living, growing enterprise. Any function can become stale over time if its sponsors become self-satisfied, overconfident, or content with the status quo.

Hold a postmortem

Plan in advance to hold a postmortem as soon as possible after the current year's event is over. It is important to do it immediately because memories dim and impressions fade. You want your members who participated in the event to recall every observation they made that could improve your future efforts.

Make it a membership meeting that involves all who participated, not just the officers and committee chairmen. Discuss frankly, but without individual accusation or criticism, the balls that were dropped, the errors that were made, the opportunities that were missed, the elements that failed to live up to expectations and those whose popularity was underestimated. Invite suggestions from your members on how the deficiencies might be remedied next year. Solicit suggestions for new activities that might be added to future events, and determine whether some elements should be eliminated which have lost popularity because they have become stale with repeated use.

Next, evaluate your organizational structure. Did you have enough committees, the right committees, too many committees? Were too many workers assigned to one task and not enough to another? Could additional tasks have been assigned, or different procedures employed, to make the event proceed more smoothly?

Now, make a list of all those outside the organization who donated money, merchandise, advertising, food, publicity, time, energy, and anything else that contributed to the success of the event. Make sure you don't miss anyone, and assign responsibility to see that everyone on the list receives a personal "thank you" note. Tell them how much money you raised with their help, and stress the significance of the ways in which the money will be spent. Keep this list because you may want to seek their help again next year.

It is amazing how thoughtless some organizations are about

acknowledging donations, and how inefficient they can be in following up on past donors in subsequent years. Frequently donors give generously in response to appeals and don't receive a word of thanks in return. This sort of discourtesy or inefficiency is inexcusable in any organization. Not only is it bad manners, but individuals who have already supported your cause should be the prime source of future help. They probably won't be if you fail to extend the courtesy of acknowledging their gift. They won't be, either, if you fail to keep accurate donor records and consequently fail to request another donation the following year.

Duties of outgoing chairman

Experience is a great teacher, and those who have the experience can be great teachers. It should be the responsibility of your outgoing chairman to indoctrinate his or her successor, sharing the experience gained. It is also an obligation to prepare detailed records to guide the successor. They should include complete and precise organizational details, an accounting of problem areas and how to deal with them, and any other information that will assure that past mistakes are not repeated, and that the incoming chairman will not have to reinvent the wheel.

The outgoing chairman should be responsible for seeing that all of your lists are brought up to date: Lists of committee chairmen and members, members with special skills, merchants and others who donated merchandise and services, benefactors who contributed cash, spouses who have special talents or access to special services that you require and, finally, the mailing list of those who have attended previous events.

If you do all of these things you will have begun to lay the foundation for another successful event. The next stone in that foundation should be an occasion that will inspire your members to do it all over again.

It's time to throw a party!

If you have heeded the previous advice about the importance of recognizing exceptional individual effort, you will have laid plans for some form of recognition of those members whose performance was outstanding. Wrap a cocktail party, dinner, and/or dance around an "Award Night," attended by husbands and wives, at which the accolades will be distributed.

This should be a fun event, but that doesn't mean you should treat it lightly. You want to emphasize the significance of the awards so that your top performers will feel rewarded, and so that the others present will covet the awards and try to earn one next year.

If your benefit was for the support of a charitable institution or organization, ask a top spokesman for the beneficiary to attend your dinner and tell the members what their efforts will mean to the people they helped. If you are supporting some controversial social issue, have a leading spokesman for that cause present to inspire your group.

Most of all, make the occasion really special, so that everyone has a memorable time. Even though they are still exhausted by their recent efforts (and perhaps by the party, too), if you do this successfully your members will be ready and eager to go to work to outdo themselves next year. While they're still glowing from the party, and brimming with the pride and joy of achievement, draft the timetable and begin assigning responsibilities for the year ahead!

8

Going after
the heavy hitters

Although corporations and foundations provide only a fraction of the charitable support contributed in the nation each year, the total is still in the billions. It can be very important to organizations that successfully solicit this category of givers. Benefit events that you sponsor and individual solicitation may remain your major source of income, but one contribution of a thousand dollars or more equals an awful lot of bingo cards or chicken dinners.

There are literally hundreds of thousands of businesses in the country that make contributions in amounts varying from a hundred dollars or so to multi-millions of dollars a year. In addition, there are more than 26,000 foundations, many of which also make contributions that run into the millions of dollars a year. These include nearly 400 large general purpose foundations that control about two-thirds of foundation assets and make about the same percentage of the grants. Then there are special purpose foundations which restrict their grants to specific areas of giving; corporate or company foundations controlled and operated by business corporations; family foundations controlled or operated for the family that created them; and community foundations that are actually consortia of living donors, trusts, endowments, and so on. They manage funds for donors in accordance with individual stipulations and pool the remaining funds that are entrusted to their discretion for distribution to charities that they investigate and select. The San Francisco Foundation and the Chicago Community Trust are examples of this type of foundation.

If you intend to take on the corporations and foundations you should begin with a clear understanding that the competition is fierce, and that it comes from national organizations, colleges and universities, major cultural institutions, and other groups and institutions that usually employ full-time development officers and are prepared to spend substantial sums to prove their case. You probably can't afford a paid development officer but you can duplicate most of what your competitors do by using volunteers. And you must approach the task with professionalism if you hope to impress the heavy hitters and compete effectively.

This does not apply if your group is small and if you intend only to solicit smaller business organizations that have an interest in you because you are working directly in the community where they operate. You may enjoy success with these firms simply by writing a letter to the president or owner describing your objectives, stating your needs, and requesting a small donation. If the amount is not large they probably will not go to the trouble of making an extensive investigation of your group, particularly if there are some recognizable names on your letterhead.

Another approach, with a neighborhood manufacturing corporation or other larger business, is to call the public relations department and ask for advice on how to solicit a contribution from the company. This may yield a check with no further effort, or lead to an appointment for a personal solicitation. This can also be done by letter, but it is easier to say "no" to a letter than to a real, live person on the telephone or sitting across the desk.

But let's assume that you want to try to reach the heavy hitters—the corporations and foundations that have the potential of providing your organization with $1,000 or more. Let's begin by taking a look at what they have come to expect of the organizations they support.

What major donors expect of you

Most large givers subscribe to the reporting and advisory service offered by the National Information Bureau, Inc. (NIB), in New York. This organization, which also supplies research on individual charitable groups, has established a set of guidelines for giving. Individual subscribers may modify them somewhat, but if you attempt to comply with these guidelines you should meet the requirements of most major donors.

The NIB lists eight standards for what it describes as "wise giving." Many of them are applicable only to the large national charitable organizations, such as those in the health field, but all will be included here and your group can apply those that fit its operations.

1. *Board of directors*—The organization should have an active and responsible governing body which serves without compensation, meets regularly, and exercises effective administrative control. Paid staff members and others who receive direct or indirect compensation as the result of board decisions should not serve as members.

2. *Purpose*—The organization should have a clearly defined statement of purpose that focuses on a legitimate need and does not waste philanthropic resources by duplicating the efforts of others.

3. *Program*—The organization should demonstrate reasonable management efficiency with adequate material and per-

sonnel resources to carry out its stated program, plus reasonable administrative and fund-raising expense. (Any major giver will be turned off by a group that devotes an excessive percentage of its receipts to administrative and fund-raising costs.)

4. *Cooperation*—Organizations should consult and cooperate with the established agencies in the same and related service fields, and determine what services are being provided by others before embarking on new programs.

5. *Ethical promotion*—Only ethical methods of publicity, promotion, and solicitation of funds should be used by the organization. It should not exaggerate, mislead, or make false claims about its accomplishments. Financial claims made in its literature should agree with the financial results reported in its audited financial statements.

6. *Fund-raising practice*—The organization should not pay commissions for fund raising, mail unordered tickets or merchandise with a request for payment, do general telephone solicitation, or use persons identified as government employees in solicitation of the public. If professional fund raisers are used they should be paid on a flat fee, not a commission basis.

7. *Audit*—New organizations should provide an independent certified public accountant's statement that a proper financial system has been installed. All organizations should provide an annual audit employing Uniform Accounting Standards and prepared by an independent certified public accountant, showing all support/revenue and expenses in reasonable detail.

8. *Budget*—The organization should prepare a detailed annual budget, consistent with the Uniform Accounting Standards employed in the audit report, which translates program plans into financial terms. The budget should be approved by the board of directors, but may be reviewed by them if there are variations during the year in the income that was projected.

These standards should be taken into consideration when

your organization approaches a major contributor. If you fall short in any area, corrective measures should be taken before you take your first major fund-raising step, which is the preparation of a specific written proposal. Let's assume that you have developed a clear statement of purpose, and that you have put your legal and financial house in order. What are the elements of an effective proposal?

Writing an effective proposal

The purpose of your proposal is to impress the donor with the goals of your organization and your competence to achieve them, and then to inspire a desire to participate. But, although you must first sell the total organization, your best approach with most major givers is to request support for a specific, identifiable project, rather than for the ongoing administration of the organization itself. Most foundations and corporations prefer to associate themselves with an innovative new project, which has a terminal point, rather than to commit themselves to supporting the continuing operating budget of the organization.

Remembering, now, that your proposal is really a sales tool, open it with a clear and dramatic statement of the need you are trying to fill. Why is your program important? Who will benefit from it? A child welfare organization, for example, might begin by describing the plight of a large number of homeless children. It would point out the damage to the children and the resulting cost of this neglect to society, currently and over a long period of time. It might equate the dollars required to correct the situation with the infinitely larger sums required from taxpayers to cover the costs of failure to meet the children's present needs.

The second section of the proposal will cover the goals and objectives of the specific project that the organization wishes to undertake. It will describe how the project will be carried out and the basis upon which the organization believes that it will achieve the desired and expected results.

The next section will describe your basic organization, cite some of its past accomplishments, and include some detail regarding individual members of the professional staff and their qualifications. This section will also list the names and affiliations of your board of directors, and perhaps include the names of other foundations and corporations that are already lending financial support. You should impress the prospective donor with the fact that you have a competent, well-staffed organization, supervised by a strong outside board of directors, which has already won the support of significant donors.

Now insert a description of the methods you propose to use to evaluate your project as it proceeds and when it has been completed. Donors want to be assured, when they invest in a new project, that provisions have been made to measure the results. Without provision for continuing evaluation a project can run for years without any real assurance that it is accomplishing the purpose for which it was intended.

Hopefully, if you have done your work well, you have now captured the interest of the donor. He is aware of the need, sympathetic to your desire to do something about it, and persuaded that you have identified a project that will help. You have also convinced him that your agency has the capability to carry it out.

Elements of an effective budget

This will lead to the detailed budget that you have prepared for the project. The budget will give income and expenses. The income side will show the receipts you anticipate receiving or are attempting to raise, including the source; the expense side will include, at a minimum, salary costs of each position, fringe benefits, rent, utilities, telephone, equipment, office supplies, printing, postage, travel, consultant expense, and a miscellaneous category.

Your budget projection will reveal the total cost of your

project, the amount already on hand, and the sum that still needs to be raised. State that the organization hopes to receive a specific portion of this amount from the donor you are approaching. Wrap it up with a summary of the proposal, emphasizing the benefits to be gained from the project—to the public and to those who fund it.

As an appendix to your proposal, attach any backup material that you believe will support your cause. This could include newspaper and magazine clippings describing some of your more important achievements or reflecting the opinions others hold of you. You may wish to include a brochure describing your organization, if one is available, a copy of your last annual report, a copy of your most recent certified public audit, and a copy of your IRS determination letter.

Your proposal is now complete. If you have done it well it will evoke sympathy for your cause, approval of your project, respect for your administrative and managerial skills and professional talents, and admiration for the cost-effectiveness of your budget. It is concise, respecting the time pressures that are on the reader, frank and honest, clear and unadorned with self-serving generalities.

It is, in short, a document that will make the reader impatient to part with his money!

9

How to be a beggar and enjoy it

The solicitation of individual donors, for most people, is an onerous and even frightening chore—one to escape or postpone. It is a natural reaction, because most of us are at least mildly ill at ease when meeting strangers. Small wonder that we should avoid situations in which, on first exposure, we must not only try to impress someone new to us, but ask him for money, too.

Often, in fund raising, our reluctance is compounded because the types of people who can be expected to give the most are often those we may hold somewhat in awe. In many cases, they have important titles and control enormous wealth. They're the people who are always in the papers, receiving an honor or associating casually with another celebrity. They often project an image of power and authority which may seem overwhelming. "How on earth," you ask yourself, "can *I* go to *him* and ask for money?"

Most of us are also reluctant to place ourselves in potentially embarrassing situations. Once we have been assigned to make a fund-raising call we begin to imagine what the scene will be like. What if we find that we can't adequately answer all the questions that are raised? What if the prospective donor is rude, or becomes angry? The negative image of these consequences is enough to prompt further delay during which our fear of the encounter mounts even further. Rarely does it occur to us that we are constantly being solicited for donations ourselves and don't react as we fear our intended target will.

Finally, no one likes to fail, so most of us avoid challenges when the outcome is uncertain. Our subconscious concern is with our own image. If our peers know that we were entrusted with an important assignment and failed, our status in our own group is impaired.

Your members must overcome fear

It is imperative, if your group is to do successful solicitation, that your members overcome this hangup. There is no effective substitute for face-to-face solicitation of funds. True, it is easier for the solicitor to write a letter than to face the prospective donor, but—as suggested earlier—it is also easier for the donor to say "No!" to a letter than to someone who is facing him on the other side of his desk. He knows that the solicitor has volunteered to make the call as a socially responsible act which required the sacrifice of time that could have been spent more pleasantly. Because failure is a waste of the solicitor's time, he'll feel impelled to respond positively if it is at all possible for him to do so. He is not under that kind of pressure when he can dispose of the matter simply by ignoring or dictating a negative reply to a letter.

Given the urgent necessity of face-to-face fund raising, how can you overcome the normal aversion many of your members will have to personal solicitation? There are several things you can do to make the task less appalling to them.

Let's assume that your objective is to obtain a grant for your organization from the president of the Mammoth Steel Corporation Foundation. You should begin by making a careful study of the foundation itself and the individual executive you intend to approach. Better still, your organization should develop a structured way of doing this in the case of Mammoth Steel and all the other prospective major donors in your community. Some of the most effective nonprofit organizations are those that have created a Research and Evaluation Committee for this purpose. Typically, this is a committee composed of affluent and knowledgeable people who are not awed by wealth or power, and who have the "connections" to obtain the information they need.

The purpose of this committee is threefold:

First, it will survey the local philanthropic field and identify the major donors. This can be accomplished, in part, on the basis of personal knowledge, but the committee will also use one or more of the other available resources. They include the Foundation Directory, the Foundation Quarterly, and the Foundation Grants Index, all of which should be available in your local library, or the Regional Library of the Foundation Center. Having done this, the committee will make a detailed analysis of the philanthropic interests of each donor, and reduce its list to those that have an interest in the type of project you will ask them to support. There's no point in wasting the time of your solicitors on an effort to secure a contribution for an environmental activity from a foundation whose known interests are limited to child welfare or education.

Second, the committee will evaluate the giving pattern of each donor to determine how much he should be expected to give. It is dangerous to ask for an unreasonably large amount because the donor may find it more comfortable to say "No" than to offer a substantially smaller sum and fear that he may appear "cheap." But it is also risky to ask for too little, and demean the donor or expose your own lack of preparation by underestimating his potential. If your committee does its homework well, and investigates the level of support the prospective donor has given to other organizations, it should be able to determine the optimum amount that a donor can be expected to contribute.

Third, the committee should study the attitudes, likes and dislikes of the individual who will be approached. This will determine the arguments that will be most appealing to him and also help you select a team of solicitors with whom he is most likely to have personal rapport.

Note that I didn't say *solicitor.* I said *team,* and a team of two it should be, so that they can give moral support to each other, as well as share defeat if that is what—despite all of your preparations—it turns out to be. The members you select will accept the assignment less reluctantly because the committee's work has already raised their confidence level. They can undertake the assignment knowing (1) that the prospective donor is sympathetic to your cause and has given to similar organizations in the past; (2) that the amount to be requested is appropriate and consistent with previous gifts that he has made; and (3) that the donor is "their kind of guy" and they were picked for the solicitation because they and the prospect could be expected to get along well together.

Involve solicitors in drafting proposal

In the previous chapter we discussed the drafting of the basic proposal. When you have decided on a specific prospect it should be reviewed and modified in any way your Research and Evaluation Committee believes will increase its appeal to the donor you intend to visit. The solicitors should be involved in this review so that they will be thoroughly familiar with the contents of the proposal, and the reasons for any modifications that are made. This will help them to determine the elements of the proposal that they should highlight during the discussion. It will also help to raise their confidence level.

The next step in the confidence-building process is to conduct a dry run of the interview. Have a member of the Research and Evaluation Committee, or some other member, pose as the prospective donor. Ask the solicitors every embarrassing or difficult question that might conceivably come up in the course of the real interview. This serves two purposes. It ensures that the solicitors won't be confronted with a question that they can't handle, and thus fail to make the sale. It also gives confidence to the solicitors by eliminating their concern that they may be confronted with and embarrassed by questions that they can't answer.

Arranging for the interview

With this preliminary effort completed and your troops ready for battle, it is time to arrange a meeting with the victim. You can accomplish this simply by writing a letter or making a phone call requesting an appointment, but there is a better way. Call on your Research and Evaluation Committee again and ask them to identify a friend or associate of the donor who will arrange the appointment for you. This also adds to the confidence of the solicitors, who no longer have to confront the donor "cold." Once in his office, they can open the conversation with a reference to the mutual friend who arranged the appointment. Meanwhile, the donor will be more receptive because he believes that he would not have been asked to grant the interview if the friend who arranged it did not believe that your mission was important and worthy.

If your solicitors are novices, arrange one last briefing session before they conduct the solicitation. Remind them of the importance of being on time. Busy executives schedule their day by the clock, and you don't want your volunteers to arrive late and discover that their prospect is already well into his next appointment. This may seem to be a needless caution, but it is not. Often the volunteers who solicit money for nonprofit groups are without experience in the business world and consequently don't place the same premium on promptness.

Although your solicitors will undoubtedly try to ease into the discussion with some preliminary conversation—perhaps about the mutual friend who arranged the appointment— caution them not to let this get out of hand. They asked for the appointment, and their host will expect them to come to the point. They should not waste his time or use up the time allotted to them with an excess of unproductive conversation.

Remind them also that in their efforts to part the donor from some of his money they are really acting as salesmen, and all of the proven sales techniques have value in this situation, as well. In fact, a few hours with a couple of good books on the art of selling is useful preparation for a solicitation interview. The most important trick is ages old, but it still works. Try to steer the conversation in ways that get the prospect in the habit of saying "Yes." You can do this by making statements and asking questions that make agreement inescapable. If your prospect has said "Yes" repeatedly throughout the interview it is difficult for him to revert to "No" when the time comes to close the sale.

The most important thing for the solicitor/salesman to keep in mind is the need to make a good impression as a person in order to get an attentive reception for your message. Solicitors should be unfailingly courteous and completely frank and honest. They should exhibit great sincerity in dramatizing the significance of the organization's mission, emphasizing the skill and efficiency with which it pursues its objectives and the prudence it exercises in the management of its funds.

Finally, they must "close the sale." Never terminate an interview without attempting to reach some conclusion. Ideally, that conclusion will be an assurance of support, but this is not always possible. In the case of a foundation executive director, for example, he may not be empowered to make a decision in behalf of his board. Nevertheless, you can try to obtain his assurance that he will make a vigorous presentation in your behalf before that board.

If no definite assurance is forthcoming don't fail to keep the contact alive by arriving at a mutual understanding that you will follow up within some specific period of time. Don't allow your prospect to believe that he will be allowed to avoid a decision, one way or the other. If the interview is left hanging on an indecisive note, with no provision for follow-up, it may be hung up forever.

Not all of your interviews will be successful, of course, but if you follow the guidelines given here many of them will. And each time you'll experience the warm glow of achievement that will make you eager to take on your next prospect!

10

Play it again, Sam!

Before we go on to specific fund-raising projects, let's review some of the basic rules of successful fund raising that have been covered in the last nine chapters. Keep them in mind as you explore the options that are offered in the chapters ahead. Remember, though, that these admonitions must be applied selectively. Not all of them will apply to all organizations or all events, because of differences in membership, size, and objectives. Observe those that apply to your group.

Keep in mind, too, as you consider the fund-raising options that are offered, that while you want to raise as much money as possible it should not be an unpleasant chore that you are involved in only out of a sense of duty. Try to select an event that suits the talents, interests, and personalities of your membership. Some groups will find a garden walk exciting, and a bingo party a colossal bore. Others couldn't care less about hydrangeas, but find fascination in the atmosphere of a bingo game. The gardeners shouldn't pick bingo for their event, or vice versa, because then neither group will have any fun.

The odds are that the events that will produce best for you are those that will yield pleasure for both members and guests. Don't forget, once you have made the selection, to plan auxiliary events for your members that will contribute to its success and be fun for them. Try to manage the event on a participatory basis, so your members will feel they are part of the decisions as well as the work. Don't put square pegs in round holes; match work assignments to the special talents and interests of each individual volunteer. And finally, be sure to share credit and reward your workers for outstanding effort.

Reminders about organization

Unless your organization is merely a loose-knit neighborhood social group whose fund-raising efforts are incidental, be sure to establish your organization on a firm legal basis. Pay close attention to legal requirements and particularly to any financial obligations you may have to the IRS.

Develop an effective organizational structure, with a strong slate of officers and committees that are appropriate for the efforts you plan to undertake. Recruit a strong board of directors, preferably one with stature in the community, and don't neglect your efforts to develop a strong membership base. Try to select events that will yield new members as well as money.

Develop a sound budget that relates expenditures to income, establish an effective accounting system, and make provision for an annual audit of your books. Manage your financial assets carefully. Don't plan activities that require a substantial upfront investment unless you are certain they will be profitable; have backup resources in your treasury to cover the costs in the event of failure. Don't sign contracts for guarantees or other expenses if failure of the event would make it impossible for you to live up to the contract. Invest surplus cash wisely, and don't make unsecured loans unless the survival of your organization depends on it.

Write a strong statement of purpose for your organization and develop short- and long-range plans for achieving your objectives. Communicate your objectives to the public, and report on the progress you make toward achieving them, so the public will know that the contributions you receive are accomplishing worthy purposes.

Identify your short- and long-range financial needs and fund-raising goals, and develop a timetable for your fund-raising program that will assure you of the cash flow needed to operate your organization. Pinpoint responsibility for every element that is necessary to achieve success.

Fund-raising project selection

In developing your fund-raising program, plan an event or series of them that will yield the amount of money required to meet the objectives of your organization. Involve your members in the selection process so they will feel a personal commitment to the success of the event. Try to select fund-raising projects that will publicize the goals of your group and attract new members, as well as meet your financial objectives.

Be sure, in selecting a project, that it is one that matches the volunteer human resources and talents that are available in your group. You won't make any money trying to conduct an event that requires talents and resources you can't provide, or that is simply too big for your group to handle. A small success is always better than a large failure!

Study your community to determine the types of events that have the greatest appeal to the market you are trying to reach. Look at competing events that are conducted annually or even more frequently. Could be yours will be one bazaar too many. Watch your timing, and avoid situations in which an event that might have been successful fails because you didn't give yourself sufficient lead time to plan and develop it properly. Finally, try to be creative. Pay attention to what's "in" this year, and even if you are planning a traditional type of event, look for ways to make it fresh, novel, and exciting.

Managing your project

The success of your event will depend upon the selection of a hard-working chairman who is able to inspire comparable effort from others. He or she should be well-organized and attentive to details. He or she should be firm but not domineering, decisive but not arbitrary, understanding but not lax, modest and confident.

The chairman, with the involvement of the membership, will develop a committee structure that is adequate for the event you plan. Responsibilities will be divided among committees so that all of the work gets done by committees that feel neither underutilized nor overburdened. Every volunteer will feel that her services are valued and recognized by the chairman and the other members of the group.

Match the tasks to be performed with the talents that are available, but make a special effort to enlarge your resources by looking for help outside your group. Avoid expenditures for materials or services that, with a little effort, you might get for free. Think creatively about potential sources of outside help.

Don't let your publicity program fall between the chairs. Select one of your most competent members to head this activity—one with the energy and interest to learn to do the job professionally. All of your planning and effort will be wasted if you fail to merchandise your event effectively.

Don't underutilize the resources of your organization because you are too timid to take on a significant project. Some groups with the potential to raise substantial sums fail to do so because they fail to look beyond their own membership. They simply feed on themselves, raising only the money that is available internally instead of attracting the contributions of others.

Give the public value received from every event that you conduct and don't try to exact exorbitant profits by charging unreasonable fees. You want your guests to return next year and *bring* their friends, rather than stay away and *warn* their friends.

Be ethical and honest in everything you do. Nonprofit groups should be purer than snow. One major national organization learned this when it was caught falsifying the records of the number of people it served. A Chicago group learned it when they falsified records that verified the number of miles kids had ridden in a Bike-A-Thon. How does a respectable charitable group survive the revelation that it has encouraged kids to cheat?

We're ready now to move on to the events themselves. You'll find them organized by categories—audience participation events, events involving food and drink, others at which merchandise is sold, entertainment and sports events, and so on. In most cases you will find the description of a basic type of event, and then the many variations you might consider. As you read the descriptions make a note of those which you believe your members might enjoy and which your group has the talents and resources to handle. Then go through the list again and select a smaller number of the most attractive possibilities. This will give you a list from which your membership can arrive at a final selection.

Happy hunting!

11

Audience
participation events

Events in which the public has an opportunity to participate
are among the most popular and profitable of fund-raising
occasions. These include carnivals, at which the public enjoys
rides and games, or tours and exhibitions where the guests can
move around rather than being anchored in a seat. It is not
unusual for some of these fund raisers to gross in excess of
$100,000, as was the case with the Showcase House presented
by the Women's Association of the Morristown Memorial
Hospital, in New Jersey. The membership spent 18 months,
working with local interior designers, to prepare the Geral-
dine Rockefeller Dodge house for public display, but when it
was over they had raised $260,000!

Most groups, of course, do not have the human or financial
resources to undertake a project of this magnitude, but that
doesn't stop them from making big money in their fund-
raising activities. The Chicago chapter of the Kiwis, an
association of former American Airlines flight attendants,

79

proved that in their efforts to aid the Park Lawn Association for Retarded Children. Over a 15-year period, although the group has only 100 members, they raised more than $100,000 by organizing fashion shows, theater parties, dinner dances and other events that could be handled by a group of that size.

Perhaps your group has a more limited objective and wishes only to put together a specific community project. If so, it might follow the example of another Chicago group, the parents of children at the Nettelhorst Elementary School. In 1976, disturbed that the school's asphalt play yard contained nothing but a couple of broken swings, they decided to do something about it. The officers of the school's PTA approached Richard Fogelman, an architectural instructor at the University of Illinois Chicago Circle campus, and sought his help.

Fogelman turned the problem over to his first-year design classes, and they began to work with the parents and teachers to design a new play yard. Then, over a two-year period, the parents sponsored Halloween carnivals, theater benefits, and other small events to raise $2,000 for trees, paint, and construction materials. They furnished the labor themselves. Today, a huge mural adorns the wall of the school adjacent to the play area. The ugly asphalt has been painted with a design created by the students—green, yellow, and bright blue—that breaks the play yard up into small areas so that the children now play in small groups, rather than racing dangerously over the entire area. Thirty green ash and honey locust trees have been planted, a sand area installed, and the parents are now working on climbing equipment constructed of old railroad ties and rubber tires.

Whatever your resources and monetary goals, you'll find ideas you can use in the pages that follow.

Decorators' showcase

A showcase house like the one presented so successfully by

the ladies in Morristown capitalizes on the pride most people take in their homes, and their desire for ideas to improve them. Developing one requires the cooperation of your local interior decorators, a house they can decorate, and an enormous amount of work in making the arrangements, supervising the project, publicizing it, and selling tickets.

Most organizations that undertake a showcase house do so in cooperation with the local chapter of the American Society of Interior Designers (ASID), which has cooperated in developing hundreds of these projects in cities all over the United States. The interior designer's interest, of course, and that of the cooperating merchants who supply the furnishings, is in displaying their wares to a large number of potential customers whom they otherwise might not reach. If your group has the resources to organize and manage a Showcase House, and you live in an affluent area with good customer potential, you may be able to secure the cooperation of your local ASID members in staging such an event.

The typical showcase house is a stately mansion that holds interest of itself because of its history and size. In 1978 the Lake County Region chapter of the Women's American Organization for Rehabilitation Through Training (ORT) developed an "International Design House" in Highland Park, Illinois. The organization secured the use of an elegant mansion situated on a high bluff overlooking Lake Michigan. The house is a copy of an Italian villa which its builder, wealthy grain broker Edward Lichtstern, had once seen overlooking the Mediterranean. The palatial residence has a 45-foot living room, a 24 by 45-foot library, and a "fainting room" and "smoking room" adjacent to the ballroom on the third floor.

The ORT group made the legal arrangements for its use, and 20 members of the Chicago chapter of ASID took on the task of decorating the home's 27 rooms. It took a year of preparation to put the home on display for three weeks, but when it had been completed thousands of visitors trooped through it at $4 per person to view the Tiffany table setting in the eighteenth-century English Adam dining room, and the diverse treatment of the other rooms of the house.

Revenues from the exhibit were not limited to the admission fees. The ORT women served luncheon in the ballroom, featuring a fashion show staged by four Chicago department stores. A "Boutique Unique," featuring handmade craft items, was housed in the basement. And to make sure that no potential customers were turned away by the lack of parking space, a shuttle bus service was operated to a nearby church parking lot.

Clearly, a project of this magnitude is one only a substantial organization would dare undertake. Moreover, depending upon the houses that are available—whether you can borrow one or have to buy it—the initial investment in a showcase house can be substantial. Yet, it is also possible to do it on a smaller scale. The Oak Park/River Forest Infant Welfare Society did so when they cooperated with the Illinois ASID to decorate "The Story Book House," a four-bedroom residence occupied by concert pianist Paul Aurandt and his wife.

House tours

Most of us have an insatiable curiosity about the manner in which others live, particularly those who enjoy the affluence that we aspire to. Yet, short of risking arrest as a Peeping Tom, few of us have the opportunity to visit the homes of the Great Gatsbys of our era, unless we sign up for a house tour. Fortunately for the charitable organizations in America, many of us do.

House tours also appeal to persons looking for decorating ideas, and to those who are planning to build a home and are seeking architectural ideas. They come in infinite variations, are relatively easy to organize and manage, and do not require a significant investment up front. With some persuasion, you can probably find local merchants who will donate needs such

as insurance coverage, ticket printing, and flowers to decorate
the homes. The main concern will be to find appealing homes
whose owners are willing to open them to the public.

Many groups conduct house tours that provide bus transportation for the guests, which is included in the price of the
ticket. Others sell tickets but expect the guests to provide their
own transporation. Frequently, if the owner will permit it, a
boutique is set up in one or more of the houses to increase the
revenue from the event. This can be very profitable during the
weeks preceding the Christmas holiday.

The typical house tour will include four or five of the
statelier mansions in your community, preferably those that
are exceptionally well-decorated, or the product of a famous
architect. But, at the other end of the scale, a tour conducted
each spring by Psi Iota Xi, in Brown County, Indiana,
features eight log cabins. All of the homes on your tour do
not have to be huge. A well-decorated smaller home, which
appears grand because the furnishings have been carefully
scaled to the size of the home, sometimes is the most popular
house on the tour. That's because most of the guests live in
smaller homes, and enjoy seeing a house that demonstrates the
potential of their own.

Often, house tours are organized around a theme. A group
in Glenview, Illinois, conducts a tour called "Artists at Work,"
which takes the guests to the home studios of artists in the
area. A Jewish Historical Society sponsors bus tours through
three Chicago Jewish neighborhoods. In other communities
tours are organized that feature homes notable for the architect
who designed them, or because of their historic significance.
Another variation is a walking tour that takes the participants
to downtown locations in major cities where the architectural
and historic significance of major buildings is described, or to
public and private art galleries. Some tours adopt a theme
limited to specific rooms in the houses—a kitchen tour, for
example, or tours that are limited to dining rooms. If you're
willing to work a bit harder, you might also try a tour of

homes decorated in various themes. One group conducts one in which individual houses are decorated for Christmas, a birthday party, a baby shower, a wedding reception, and a party for children on Halloween.

Garden walks

Best suited to areas with large estates with professionally landscaped grounds, but with some smaller "do-it-yourself" gardens thrown in, garden walks are somewhat easier to arrange. Many owners of fine homes are less reluctant to expose their grounds to a horde of strangers than they are their houses.

The garden walk can be conducted on foot (if the homes are in close proximity), by bus, or your guests can be expected to transport themselves. Some groups tie a plant sale to the event, capitalizing on the fact that when their guests have observed the beautiful gardens maintained by others they may be inspired to buy some flowers of their own. One city group conducts a tour that features 30 gardens, and then sprinkles a variety of auxiliary events along the way—carnival games at one, a puppet show at another, and occasional refreshment centers throughout the tour.

Because many men enjoy gardening, a garden walk offers an unusual opportunity to get husbands into the fund-raising act. The Men's Garden Club of the North Shore conducts a garden walk through the gardens of the members, featuring a variety of types of gardens. From 1 to 6 on a Sunday afternoon, guests are permitted to view a patio garden, English garden, Japanese garden, vegetable garden, herb garden, and a 600-foot garden of vegetables, annuals and perennials, most of them started under lights, and 70 hanging containers.

As with the house tour, your major problem in scheduling a garden walk will be finding the gardens to walk in. Groups in some cities have solved this problem simply by persuading the members of the local garden club to open their own gardens to a tour. The garden club then determines which gardens will be included, and your members can concentrate on selling the tickets.

If it doesn't seem feasible to take your guests to the gardens, you have the option of bringing the gardens to the guests. Organize a flower show and award prizes in various categories to encourage entries. Supplement your ticket revenues by selling plants and refreshments, and swell your crowd by getting some experts to provide advice on flower arranging and plant care.

Art shows and exhibitions

The growing popular interest in original art has increased the appeal and profitability of community art shows. Artists in your area are invited to display their works and sell them to the visitors. The show can be held indoors, in a park or village square, or along the sidewalk in a busy urban shopping neighborhood. Some groups charge a modest fee for admission to the show. Others charge the artist for the display space he uses, or a commission on what he sells, and derive their income from that.

Art shows are relatively easy to organize and manage. They rise or fall on the success of a double-barreled promotion and publicity effort, first to recruit the participating artists and then to lure potential customers to the event. Art shows enjoy the greatest success if they are repeated year after year, enjoy increasing attendance, and become known to artists outside your own area. The annual show in St. Joseph, Michigan, has grown to include artists from all over the Midwest and also attracts visitors from many adjoining states. It started small, but today spreads for more than a mile in a beautiful park on the shores of Lake Michigan.

Part of the appeal to the artists, beyond the hope of selling some of their artwork, is the awarding of prizes for the best works in various classes. You will need to obtain the services of a committee of experts to do the judging. A variation that is growing in popularity because of the increased interest in photographic art are exhibits of the work of local photographers.

The big art shows do not discriminate with respect to the artists that are allowed to participate. Any artist may participate who is willing to pay the fee, and may display as many of his works as can be squeezed into his allotted space. Some groups sponsor exhibitions, rather than shows, and have their committee of judges do a preliminary screening to determine which works will be hung in the show. The revenue for an exhibition comes primarily from admission fees paid by art lovers who enjoy viewing quality work by contemporary artists.

Craft and hobby shows

Every community has its share of residents who are devoted to various hobbies and crafts—collectors of everything from stamps and coins to old beer cans, or enthusiasts of macrame, ceramics or model airplanes. Depending on the size of your community you may be able to turn a neat profit by staging a craft or hobby show. If the market is big enough, you might have a show featuring a single craft or hobby—a stamp show, for example. If you feel that there are insufficient potential visitors for a show featuring a single hobby or craft, have a general exhibition in which a variety of hobbies or crafts are displayed. Don't charge the exhibitors. You need them to attract a crowd. Charge an appropriate admission fee for those who attend.

The possibilities are endless. The Chicago Historical Society attracted 90 costume curators, educators, and designers representing 27 states and two foreign countries to a preview of its exhibition, "Eight Chicago Women and Their Fashions, 1860-1929." In the weeks that followed thousands paid a small admission charge to view the exhibit.

Consider identifying those in your community who own antique automobiles and persuade them to make their autos available for an antique car show. If there are enough of them in your community, present a show for model airplane enthusiasts. Doll house exhibits and displays of model rooms have also been popular attractions in many cities. A bit of careful research to identify the hobbies and crafts that are most popular in your area will help you decide the type you should feature to develop an appealing and profitable exhibit.

Animal shows are particularly attractive. The annual horse show is one of the social events of the season in many communities and, of course, dog and cat shows have almost universal appeal since most families own one or the other. Before you undertake one, though, make sure that there isn't already an established, competing annual event.

Dances

Dances, whether limited to members of your own group or open to guests from the entire community, have continuing appeal if you exercise your ingenuity to pick a theme that is novel and exciting. Form a committee of the "live wires" in your group and let them plan an event that will be fun for everyone. They can make the event more attractive by engaging a popular musical group, or by holding the dance in an unusual place. Your profit comes from the admission fee, food and liquor service, and other events such as a raffle or auction that are part of the evening's entertainment. Dance instructions can also be a feature of the event.

Square dances and barn dances are popular in many communities; some groups hold them out of doors, concluding the evening with a midnight barbecue or hot dog roast. The disco craze has spawned countless dance parties all over the country, some of them small affairs at which records are played and others larger events with live rock music. If you want to attract a broad age span, try mixing it up by playing some contemporary rock and some traditional dance music from the big band era.

There is almost no limit to the dances that can be built around a costume theme. Masquerade balls are still popular in some cities. Some organizations have planned events featuring historical costumes and even those representing the favorite hobbies and sports activities of the guests.

New Perspectives, a singles group in Chicago, holds regular disco dances and donates the proceeds to charity. They move from one popular discotheque to another. The Chicago Boys Clubs hold an annual "Tiffany Ball," with the cost underwritten by that renowned jewelry firm so that all of the proceeds can go to the organization. Volunteer fire companies and local police associations in many communities conduct annual dances to provide funds they can use to buy needed equipment, or support programs for the youth of the community. In many cases a huge percentage of the tickets sold for these events are "nontickets" purchased by citizens who won't attend the dance, but want to provide financial support for the activity.

Dances are not difficult to organize and operate, but be sure to watch your expenses carefully, particularly if you are engaging professional entertainment. It is obvious that the largest· crowds will be attracted if you feature "name band" entertainment, but the top groups are expensive and you don't want to find yourself owing them more than you earned at the door.

Fairs and festivals

If your group is large enough to provide the manpower needed to man it, a community fair or festival may be the event that will meet all of your financial needs. In most cities they are operated by the larger local organizations such as the service clubs or the volunteer fire department, but they are by no means limited to groups of that type. If your group is too small to manage a fair, or if your community already has a scheduled annual event, determine whether you can "piggyback" on it with an event of your own. Lake Forest Day, a traditional annual event in that Illinois north shore community, has long been a midweek holiday for the entire community. It was so successful and attracted so many visitors that the Lake Forest Police Association decided to schedule its annual dance on the same day, to take advantage of the crowds. That, in turn, led the local mental health group to establish a predance picnic for those attending the firemen's event.

Rural communities have great potential as sites for weekend community festivals. In addition to a carnival, with rides and other concessions, they often feature live entertainment, athletic contests, water fights involving local firemen, horse-pulling contests, and judging of livestock and homemaker exhibits of local farmers and residents. If another organization already sponsors such an event in your community explore the possibility that they will allow you to operate one element of it—a refreshment stand, for example—for the benefit of your group.

Ethnic events, featuring entertainment, foods, and bazaar items indigenous to other countries, are conducted in many communities. They may, as in the case of Milwaukee's Holiday Folk Fair, feature many nationalities or be limited to a single nationality. They are especially appealing in communities or urban neighborhoods populated by one predominant ethnic group.

Highwood, Illinois, a community in which a majority of the residents are of Italian origin, conducts an annual community festival with a strongly Italian flavor. Venerdi through Domenica (Friday through Sunday) the visitors are exposed to a series of events, beginning with the Miss Highwood Festival Pageant on Friday night, and continuing with performances of "Hansel and Gretel," a street dance, a festival parade, an Italian street soccer game, a water fight, and a Bocce ball tournament. There is a professional carnival, and the festival is topped off on Sunday night with square dancing and bluegrass music, followed by the awarding of the grand prize in the raffle—a trip to Italy for two.

Fairs and festivals can gross substantial sums for those organizations that are willing to invest the effort required to organize and conduct them. If yours is conducted in a self-contained location, and you offer worthwhile free entertainment, you may establish an admission charge. Otherwise, your profits will come from the carnival, games of chance, food service, and admission to specific events.

Don't overlook the possibility, exploited by many organizations, of conducting an annual festival on a smaller scale which includes a variety of fund-raising projects. Many churches sponsor festivals on their church grounds, often associated with a major holiday weekend. One such fair, conducted by the Church of the Holy Spirit, in Lake Forest, featured all of the following attractions, each calculated to extract money from the guests:

A Country Store, featuring craft items, baked goods and
    preserves
Carnival Corners, with games and rides for children
A variety of teenage activities, including a pie-eating contest
An indoor sitdown buffet luncheon in addition to an outdoor
    refreshment stand
A Second Time Around Shop, featuring used items
A flower sale
A silent auction

Carnivals

Any organization with members deeply committed to the cause it espouses can raise money within the group to the limit of the membership's ability to contribute. A major advantage of entertaining fund-raising events is the opportunity they provide to obtain funds from people who have no interest in your cause, but participate only for their own amusement. Sponsorship of professional carnivals offers a dramatic example of this kind of event which can, in a heavily populated area, literally gross hundreds of thousands of dollars.

The secret of success is to identify a good location in a busy area with ample parking and public transportation, and then find a reputable professional carnival operator who will provide good carnival dates. Long holiday weekends, when many people are looking for things to do, are the best.

You will want, if you sponsor a carnival, to publicize and promote it heavily, but a highly visible location is even more important. Why? If you've ever driven by carnival grounds with a brilliantly lit Ferris wheel turning against the background of a dark night sky, and heard your children shout, "Look! Look! Let's stop there!" you know why. Carnivals generate a lot of spontaneous business from motorists who "just happen to drive by."

Some groups sponsor carnivals in which all of the rides, games, and other concessions are provided by the carnival operator. They get a percentage of the take. Others contract only for the rides and perhaps some sideshows, and operate the other concessions themselves. The latter is more profitable, of course, because you keep all the profits from the concessions and still get a commission on the rides. But it also takes much more organizing and far more work.

If you elect to operate the concessions yourselves, don't overlook the profits to be made from the sale of candy, popcorn, cotton candy, soft drinks, and simple foods like hot dogs and hamburgers. Consider holding a bazaar, featuring handmade craft items, in connection with the event. If you schedule a fireworks display late each evening it will increase your profits because your customers will wait to see it, and spend money to keep busy while they're waiting.

A variation of the carnival which many smaller organizations turn to is the backyard carnival featuring homemade games. The Muscular Dystrophy Association has established the potential of these small neighborhood carnivals by providing free kits that include set-up tips, tickets, booth decorations, badges, posters, and other items. In 1977 this association involved 120,000 kids in 43,000 backyard carnivals and raised $1,500,000.

Las Vegas Night

Many upright citizens who wouldn't consider a trip to Las Vegas or the local racetrack nevertheless have a sublimated urge to gamble. They, along with the real gamblers, constitute a huge potential audience for a charity-sponsored Las Vegas Night. Your guests experience the thrill of gambling, but do it for prizes instead of money, and are comforted by the knowledge that it was all for a good cause.

Groups that sponsor Las Vegas Nights obtain the standard gambling games—blackjack tables, roulette wheels, wheels of fortune, crap tables—from carnival suppliers and then set up a casino in a large auditorium or gymnasium. The room is decorated and lighted to establish the casino "mood." Liquor may or may not be served and simple food service is available.

Guests at these events pay an admission fee at the door and are given a supply of play money which they can use at the tables. When they run out they buy a new supply from the cashier. A dollar buys one hundred dollars worth of play money, so that the players can feel like big-time gamblers without spending that much.

The gamblers are tempted by a display of prizes which can be purchased with "play money" at the end of the event. The prizes are solicited from local merchants and individuals who have been persuaded to support the event. Often, a number of major prizes—perhaps including a weeklong vacation trip to some exotic destination—are auctioned at the end of the evening. The big winners use their play money to vie with each other in bidding for each item, and the nonwinners can participate by buying more play money with which to bid.

A more elaborate variation of the Las Vegas theme is one in which the classrooms of a local school are converted into a series of restaurants and nightclubs featuring many kinds of ethnic foods and offering a variety of amateur entertainment. The event may include gambling, but often doesn't. Visitors to these affairs return year after year to be astonished by the quality and variety of talent that is available in any group of 300 or 400 persons.

Transfiguration Parish in Wauconda, Illinois, conducts an annual affair in the church school which they call "Night Train—Coast to Coast." More than 400 people, including schoolteachers, students, parishioners and townspeople are involved in decorating the classrooms to make them appear like nightclubs, providing amateur entertainment, and serving food, taking tickets, and tending bar. Some of the nightclub acts are so popular that guests wait in line for an hour or more in order to see them.

The names of the nightclubs that have been created in past years transmit the flavor of the event: Grauman's Chinese Theater, Hot Licks 'N' Harmony, Rathskeller, Track 29, Empire Room, The Big Tent, Durty Nellie's, Padrecito's Place, The Desert Inn, Our Own Tonight Show, and It's a Good. A full-scale Broadway musical performed by amateur talent from within the group is featured in the school auditorium.

Much of the food and drink sold at the affair is donated, and cooked by members of the church. Planning for the next event begins as soon as the last one is over, and months are spent in preparing decorations for the rooms and rehearsals for the entertainment. An elaborate program book is printed which earns added revenue from advertising purchased by local merchants.

Tickets to "Night Train" are sold in advance and if you fail to buy them you won't get in because the affair is a sellout, year after year. It isn't the largest event of its kind, but in a typical year Transfiguration Parish nets more than $30,000 from the event, which is used to help pay the costs of running its school.

Fun fairs

The juvenile equivalent of the carnival is the Fun Fair, aimed at children and usually sponsored by a Boy Scout troop or other children's organization. The fairs feature homemade games of chance, at which small prizes are awarded, and concessions selling soft drinks, hot dogs, popcorn, and cotton candy. Tickets are sold at the door and used by the children instead of money.

An innovative feature of one Fun Fair is "Mr. Many-pockets," a clown whose costume is completely covered with large patch pockets. The children, in exchange for a ticket, are permitted to reach into the pocket of their choice and pull out a prize. Another group has makeup artists on hand who, in exchange for a ticket, will make up the children's faces to look like clowns.

Card parties and bingo

Many people enjoy card games and like to broaden the competition by playing with persons outside their usual group. Some organizations raise modest sums by sponsoring bridge and pinochle parties and tournaments. Chess and checker tournaments are also a possibility. In six states that permit gambling at cards, these events can include poker and other gambling games, which make them more profitable. A major advantage of this type of fund raiser is that it requires a minimum of effort and expense beyond publicity and promotion and the provision of a facility in which to play.

If your group has no compunctions about the moral aspects of gambling, it can also consider the sponsorship of bingo games, which are now legal in 36 states when conducted by nonprofit organizations. You can buy or rent the equipment and repeat the event on a weekly or monthly basis throughout the year. That's important, because bingo is a game that develops devoted followers, and if you have a gifted entertainer calling the numbers, the players will return again and again.

A variation used by some organizations is white-elephant bingo, in which the prizes are gifts donated by members or obtained from local merchants. Often these are staged as the entertainment portion of a luncheon or dinner, which also generates revenue.

Marathons

The physical fitness craze, coupled with the initial success of Bike-A-Thons many years ago, has led to an incredible variety of similar events. They come in two forms; marathons in which the sponsor profits from an entry fee, and those in which the participants enlist sponsors who pay the organization running the event a specific sum per mile, hour, lap, or whatever unit of measurement is normally used for the activity.

Currently, running is in vogue, and countless marathon events have sprung up all over the country. A celebrity Jog-A-Thon in Beverly Hills, California, was actually cancelled because so many celebrities registered that the insurance premium went out of sight. During the summer of 1978 running and jogging events in the area around Seattle, Washington, were piled one on top of the other, but why not? Joggers are indefatigable. They run every day so why not compete every week?

The Robinson newspapers in Seattle sponsored a five-mile run, the Beside the Point Road Race, and donated the three-dollar entry fees to the Ruth School for Girls in Burien, Washington. More than 3,000 runners and joggers competed in the Sound-to-Narrows road race in Tacoma. In Seattle, 1,400 runners completed the 7.2 mile Seward-to-Madison

Shore Run, and 2,100 runners the 4.7 mile Seafair Summer Run. A 10-man, 24-hour distance run in Federal Way Stadium sought to break the world's record, with the proceeds going to the Citizens for School Activities drive. Meanwhile, in Lake County, Illinois, runners were seeking to swell the coffers of Catholic Charities by competing in a 15,000-meter run.

But, popular as running is, it hasn't replaced many established varieties of marathons, and new versions are popping up every day. Young people, encouraged by sponsors who will pay in accordance with their endurance, are riding bikes, roller skating, dancing, playing volleyball, swimming, and even playing the piano.

A Disco Dancethon at Chicago's "in" discotheque, Faces, attracted more than 60 dancers to a nonstop 60-hour event. It raised more than $135,000 for programs for the retarded. The Chicago Heart Association sponsored a Swim-A-Thon in the suburban pools, with participants earning a fee for each lap, and raised $109,000. The American Cancer Society sponsors Weight-A-Thons, with dieting entrants contributing for each pound they lose.

Other events that have attracted attention, participants, and money include a 12-hour Pianomarathon, Bowl-A-Thons, Read-A-Thons, in which children generate a contribution for each book they read, Monopoly tournaments, and even a jigsaw puzzle competition in which competitors were paid by the piece.

In one city, which had a community center badly in need of sprucing up, an ingenious citizen came up with the Do-A-Thon. Participants contributed work, not money, and soon the building had been painted, the shrubbery trimmed, trees planted, and minor repairs made. The Center is now in first-class condition again!

Beauty contests

A bit passé, perhaps, but beauty contests remain popular in many communities, usually in conjunction with other events.

They work best if conducted in cooperation with local news-papers. The sponsoring club buys advertising space and then sells local merchants the privilege of being listed in the ad as a sponsor of the event. The difference between the amount collected from the merchants and the amount paid for the ad is profit for the organization. Some groups sell advertising in program books which contain descriptions and pictures of the girls who are competing in the contest.

Some smaller communities have discovered that they can raise money for charity and lure out-of-town visitors by presenting a pageant in which the whole town participates. An outstanding example is the annual William Tell Pageant staged by the residents of New Glarus, Wisconsin. They can be based on holiday themes, anniversaries, or historical events. Unless you can secure a strong commitment from several hundred people who aren't afraid of hard work, it is probably unwise to attempt such an event.

Excursions

Bus excursions to interesting sites, athletic events, and places of amusement have become popular fund raisers in many cities and are also fun for your members and guests. Many amusement parks, professional athletic clubs, museums, and theaters will grant discounts for block ticket purchases. Your group can organize an excursion and make a profit on the flat fee charged for transportation and admission. You may even include lunch or dinner in the package. The price, for most of those who attend, will probably be less than if they had packed the family into their automobile and gone on their own.

If you have a local professional baseball, football, hockey, or basketball team you can arrange packages that include the admission ticket, bus transportation, and luncheon or dinner before the game. Use a local restaurant as the departure point, and negotiate a flat rate for the group meal. You will find many fans who appreciate the convenience and freedom from traffic and parking worries that the arrangement provides. These are fund raisers that must be planned well in advance, however, because you need to arrange for good seats while they are still available. If possible, you should try to sign your guests up for the entire season, so you aren't forced to search for a new group of participants for every game.

A variation was employed by the American Cancer Society in Seattle when they sponsored a "Race for a Cure," at the Longacres track. The proceeds went to the Joseph Gottstein Memorial Research Laboratory. General admission tickets were sold for $2.50, but for $100 the more affluent guests were served dinner in the Turf Club and given an opportunity to view the art show in the Longacres Gallery.

Other options include bus tours to historic homes in your area, visits to places that are not normally open to the public (Hugh Hefner's Playboy Mansions are favorites), and even group charter airplane flights to vacation destinations.

Trade shows

Industrial and trade shows can be profitable in communities where there are not events already sponsored by the local Chamber of Commerce. Profits derive from renting booth space to exhibitors and charging an admission fee for those who attend. An enterprising Exchange Club in the East rented an armory for a trade show and sold 96 exhibit booths for $40 to $150 each. Each exhibitor also bought "exhibitor's tickets" at $15 per 100. Those who were given the tickets were admitted for 15 cents each. Those without them paid 30 cents.

Telethons

The success of some of the nationwide telethons sponsored by national organizations, such as the one Jerry Lewis hosts for the Muscular Dystrophy Association, leads many groups to consider this type of event. It is possible to conduct them on a local basis, as the members of the Women's Association of the Chicago Symphony Orchestra have demonstrated. Each year they conduct the Chicago Symphony Marathon on radio station WFMT. The event extends over a weekend and those who telephone contributions can choose premiums from a catalog that is published in *Chicago* magazine.

Despite their success, the fact remains that these events are tremendously difficult to arrange, organize, and manage, and totally unsuitable for most groups. With all the options that are at your disposal, you can probably put your time to better use and enhance your chances of success by turning to another event.

"Days"

Several national organizations enjoy success with various kinds of "days" sponsored by their local chapters. The veterans' groups have Poppy Day, the Salvation Army Doughnut Day, and other groups sell candy and other merchandise. Tag days have also been effective for some organizations. If you have a great many members, or are able to recruit numerous volunteers who are willing to stand on a street corner all day, beseeching the passersby to make a contribution, you might experience success with this kind of event. If not, forget it.

12

Merchandise events

In March, 1976, the National Fund Raising Institute published an article describing the Ramble, an annual fund-raising auction conducted by Loyola Academy, a Jesuit preparatory school for boys in Wilmette, Illinois. As a result of the article Loyola received literally hundreds of requests for more information from all over the United States, and even from Australia. Ever mindful of opportunities to make a buck, the good fathers put together a packet of materials describing the event, which they are still selling for $10.

It is not suprising that other fund raisers are interested in Loyola's auction because it has grown over the years to the point where it now, in one evening, brings in more than $300,000. Almost as important, the 1,000 guests who attend and the 200 volunteers who conduct the auction, all have a ball!

The Loyola benefit auction begins at 5 P.M. on a Saturday and ends at 1:30 A.M. on Sunday. About 1,000 items, all donated by businesses and members and friends of the school, are auctioned off. The couples who attend pay $100 each for the privilege. In addition to the opportunity to bid on the merchandise, which may range from a 1,000-pound Hereford steer to seven days at the Ocean Reef club in North Key Largo, Florida, the guests enjoy a buffet dinner at 6:30 and a breakfast buffet beginning at midnight.

A handsome printed catalog, describing the items to be auctioned, is distributed in advance of the event. These items are auctioned in four ways: 1) an oral auction at which a professional auctioneer disposes of about 150 of the more expensive articles which have the greatest appeal; 2) a silent auction in which bidders visit booths in which merchandise is grouped by type and write their bids on a bidder card; 3) a key club in which guests pay $10 to purchase a key that may open the lock on some item; and 4) a duck pond in which guests use a net to snare numbered ducks floating in a pool and receive prizes of varying value based on the number written on the duck. The top prize is $1,400.

Loyola builds excitement about the auction, and also collects merchandise to be auctioned, at a series of gift-gathering parties. Usually, these are cocktail parties sponsored by alumni or parents of students, at which the price of admission is a gift of a certain value. If you ask those who manage the affair what their secret is they'll tell you, "Do everything first class." The guests are paying $100 a couple and you want them in a warm mood, feeling that they got their money's worth. The Ramble is black tie, the food is catered, the liquor flows freely, and the result is reflected in the bids that are made during the auction.

If you want to conduct a good auction and do it well, the Loyola packet is worth the ten bucks.

Not all auctions are on so grand a scale, of course, and there are many specialized varieties and ways of conducting them. Here are some others:

Auctions

Auctions are appealing because they are exciting, competitive, offer guests an excuse to buy something they would like to have but wouldn't have bought at a store, and hold out the hope if not the reality that the bidder may get a bargain. They may be conducted as independent events, or attached to another function, such as a luncheon or dinner.

In addition to auctions of general merchandise, such as that offered at the Loyola Ramble, you can present an auction of specialized items such as art objects, crafts, or antiques. These may require more effort, because of the difficulty you will have in acquiring donated merchandise. You may also, however, accept goods for auction on consignment, taking a percentage of the final bid.

A popular event for the social set in Chicago is an auction held at a posh restaurant for the benefit of the Chicago Art Institute. The guests are delighted to pay handsomely for gowns by famous designers like Noriko and Halston. Less exclusive, but probably more fun, are Dutch auctions to which each guest brings an item that is auctioned off. Other groups have experienced success with auctions featuring the services of local celebrities. You bid for the privilege of having the mayor serve as butler at your next dinner party, or get your dishes washed for a day by a local socialite.

The National Asthma Center in Denver, Colorado, has experienced great success with Bid 'n Buy luncheon auctions conducted by its local chapters all over the country. Eight California chapters raise over $40,000 a year at luncheons of this type. The principle is simple. The Bid 'n Buy is not really an auction but a raffle in which merchandise is awarded by chance rather than bids. Each guest buys five dollars worth of small change when she arrives at the luncheon. She is also given a numbered stick representing her place at the table of ten at which she is seated. The auctioneer displays the item to be auctioned and the guests who are interested place their numbered stick in a glass on the table, along with 15 cents in change. Numbers are then drawn from two drums, one representing the table number and the other the seat number. If you have stick number seven at table number ten, and those numbers are called, you are the winner.

Most of the merchandise at a Bid 'n Buy action consists of small items donated by local merchants. If you have larger, more attractive items, you can raise the price that is required to bid. After each bid the runners collect the money from each table. A variation used, if your crowd is too large, is simply to sell the numbered stick for $5, making each guest eligible for a chance at every prize. This eliminates the delay otherwise experienced in collecting the money between bids.

The strategy essential to any type of auction is to keep things moving. If you maintain a high level of excitement the guests will be inclined to bid more generously, and everyone will have more fun.

Antique shows

Inflation has heightened interest in antiques and art objects as a hedge against the declining value of the dollar, increasing the popularity of antique and art shows throughout the country. Potential customers are attracted to antique and art shows because they can inspect the wares of many dealers, all in one place.

To conduct an antique show you must rent an exhibit hall, and enlist dealers to come and display their wares. Your success in attracting a substantial number of the better dealers will determine the profits you make from the event. You will have a better chance of attracting them if yours is a respected, well-known organization, and you conduct the show in an affluent, prestigious area.

You will profit from your antique or art show in three ways. First, you will charge each dealer a fee for his exhibit space. Second, you will levy a small charge for admission. Finally, you can profit from the sale of soft drinks, coffee, and food at the event. Make sure, however, that the guests are precluded from taking food or drink into the exhibit area. The dealers don't appreciate having it spilled on their prized merchandise.

Raffles

You know what these are. You buy or have donated a substantial prize such as an automobile, and then sell chances. If you sell enough of them you make some money. The best way to do that is to require that each of your members assume responsibility for the sale of a specific number of tickets, and hope that they all return for more. Don't overlook the opportunity to sell books of chances to the local businessmen who have your members as customers. Raffles work best if they are associated with another event so you can sell tickets on the spot.

On a smaller scale, holidays offer the opportunity to raffle a turkey or ham among your members. Turkey raffles have long been popular small fund raisers within many groups.

Rummage sales

"One man's trash is another man's treasure," so the old cliché goes. This is demonstrated thousands of times each year as groups all over the country conduct rummage sales where one family's discards are eagerly snatched up by another. Almost any group can successfully conduct a rummage sale, but the magnitude of that success will be determined by the planning and effort you put forth and the manpower you have available. If your activity is limited to a few weeks immediately in advance of the event, you cannot expect to enjoy the returns that are possible if your preparations are a year-round effort.

Besides careful planning and organization, one of the reasons for the success of the Lake Forest event mentioned earlier is the quantity and quality of merchandise available. The rummage sale is conducted throughout the church and the adjacent Sunday School building, with merchandise grouped by category so that buyers can find what they are looking for easily. One room will contain toys, another lawn equipment, another furniture, another appliances. There is a "Treasure Room" for the more valuable items and a "French Room" containing designer dresses.

The members of the First Presbyterian Women's Association who conduct the sale recognized years ago that families dispose of unwanted items throughout the year. They take advantage of this, and make certain that no merchandise gets away from them, by collecting the used items 12 months of the year. There is a storage room to which merchandise can be delivered at any time, and when the sale date arrives it is bursting at the seams. Groups that limit their collection activities to a short period of time get less merchandise of a lower quality.

The Lake Forest sale is held in early May, but as early as the previous August the church bulletin begins reminding members of the event, urging them, when they do the traditional fall cleanup around the house, to bring unwanted items to the church. A pickup service is provided for larger items. In February, efforts begin to recruit the more than 600 workers who are needed to man the sale. A four-page bulletin is mailed out, giving a schedule of events connected with the sale and listing the names and telephone numbers of all of the chairpersons. A return postcard is enclosed on which members can indicate their willingness to help, the kind of job they prefer, and the hours during which they will be willing to work. They can choose to work setting up one of 31 separate merchandise departments, as well as manning the café where workers are served coffee and hot lunches, or serving as a cashier, salesperson, wrapper, or floorwalker.

In mid-April a "Fashion and Treasure Tea" is conducted at the home of one of the members. Guests are expected to contribute one dollar and an item to be sold in the "Treasure Room." The program includes a fashion show at which gowns to be sold in the French Room are modeled. About ten days before the sale, the window display committee begins installing displays of the more attractive sale items in local store windows.

A week before the sale the chairmen and cochairmen gather for coffee at which they receive a final briefing on the efforts required during setup week and on the day of the sale. After church services on the Sunday preceding the sale, hundreds of workers begin sorting and pricing the merchandise accumulated over the previous year, and organizing the departments. This activity continues until noon on Wednesday. The workers, men as well as women, have already received postcards advising them of their assignments. A free baby-sitting service is provided for workers with small children.

By noon on Wednesday the sale is ready to go, and at 2:30 P.M. the Workers' Presale begins. The volunteers are given the privilege of shopping the sale and buying items for 20 percent more than they will be sold for on sale day. The chairmen are permitted to shop for the first hour, as a reward for the greater effort they have put forth, and then the other workers are admitted. They use their assignment cards for identification.

The workers report for duty at 6:30 A.M. on sale day, again using their assignment cards for admission. Crowds have already gathered when they arrive, and cars jam the side streets near the church. Many have driven 100 miles or more. The doors open at 7 A.M. and from then on the sale is well-organized chaos as customers race from room to room trying to snatch the choice items before they are discovered by someone else. Twelve hours later, exhausted but $50,000 richer, the workers lock the doors.

Experience has taught the Women's Association to impose strict security measures on their sale. The identification cards are used because everyone in the group doesn't know everyone else, and they don't want strangers, in the guise of workers, to slip into the sale. Nothing can be removed from the building until it has been paid for. Even the committee that removes merchandise for use in the store windows is required to sign a duplicate receipt, one copy of which is retained by the association until the merchandise is retrieved and returned.

Three hours before the end of the sale, the workers began cutting prices. In the clothing and toy departments customers are permitted, for a dollar, to take as much merchandise as they can cram into a shopping bag. An hour later the price is lowered to 50 cents, and an hour before the end of the sale, to a quarter. The theory is that anything that hasn't sold by then probably isn't going to be sold. Anything they can get for it is better than having to cart if off or give it away.

Items are priced individually, except in the clothing departments where the better items are tagged, and the remainder placed on tables bearing price signs. The clothing items are grouped so that all the men's trousers are on one table that bears a price sign for that item, all the shoes, at a different price, on another, and so on. This avoids the need to price thousands of clothing items individually.

Additional revenue is produced at the sale through the sale of refreshments, and also at a Curio Boutique which features handmade craft items and homemade bakery goods. No merchandise is carried over from 'year-to-year; unsold items are given to other charities and sold to second hand dealers. However, because there is a cutoff date beyond which items that are received will not be sorted and priced for the current year's sale, the storeroom already contains items to be sold next year before this year's event has begun.

Soon after the sale is over, the Women's Association conducts its annual Spring Luncheon to thank the workers, announce the results of the sale, and install its new officers for the coming year. That's their signal to begin working on the rummage sale to be held next year!

Your organization may not have the resources to conduct so elaborate a sale, but whatever its size, plan and organize it well. Don't settle for a jumble of merchandise scattered randomly on tables. Sort and group it carefully so that items that might have sold do not go undiscovered. Most important, be sure you have plenty of volunteers on hand to make certain that customers pay for the treasures that they discover.

Flea markets

Back in 1312, Henry II proclaimed that the peddlers who were plying their trade in the streets of London were infesting the town with fleas, and banned them to the outskirts of the city. Londoners began referring to their campsite as the "flea market." The name stuck, and the peddlers prospered. Meanwhile, across the English Channel, the ragpickers of Paris also began to gather in the northern district of the city to sell their wares. That was the beginning of *Le Marche Aux Puces*, which today includes more than 3,000 stalls spread over four square miles and has become a major tourist attraction.

The idea came to the United States in 1958, when an antique dealer named Russell Carrell staged an "Original One-Day Rural Flea Market" on marshland he owned in Salisbury, Connecticut. "I copied the name from Paris," he said. "I was working with a charity organization and the idea just came to mind."

That first American flea market had 80 dealers, but the concept has grown and spread across the country. Vacant garages, fairgrounds, parking lots are sites for flea markets, many of them charity sponsored, at which individuals paying a modest fee for space can display new or used merchandise that they wish to sell. They attract people looking for specific items that they can't afford to buy at the store, as well as wealthy antique buffs hoping to buy a bargain treasure from a dealer who is unaware of its worth.

One West Texas flea market is situated inside an abandoned 57,000-barrel oil storage tank. Others are held in abandoned theaters and outdoor theater parking lots. Perhaps the largest of them all is that conducted each month in the Rose Bowl in Pasadena, California. Nearly 100,000 people attend to inspect the merchandise offered by more than 2,000 dealers who arrive

in trucks and vans loaded with goods from as far away as
Kansas. If all the booths were lined up in a row it would be
five miles long.

You can profit from a flea market by selling space to
exhibitors and operating a refreshment stand. In addition, you
can have booths of your own and operate a sort of perpetual
rummage sale. A booth selling craft items made by your
members is also a possibility. The major requirements are
finding a good, visible location with ample parking space, and
then attracting vendors to participate. Some flea market merchants are professionals who make their living at it. And
finally, there are individuals who are selling their own unwanted possessions in order to gain a little extra spending
power for themselves. If you can find enough dealers to get
one going, and it draws good crowds, other dealers will learn
of it and it will grow under its own steam. But watch out for
fleas.

Garage sales

Garage sales began as an outlet for unwanted things that
were "too good to throw away." Many charitable groups have
adopted the idea by collecting sale items from the members of
their group and conducting a garage sale of their own. Those
who attend may be looking for a specific item, such as a used
baby bed, seeking to find quality clothing for their children at
bargain prices, hoping to spy a valuable antique that is
offered at a ridiculously low price, or simply find "garage
saling" an enjoyable way to spend their time.

Garage sales are an excellent way for a small group to raise
money, but operating one is not as simple as it seems. There
are many tricks you should keep in mind if you want to make
as much mmey as possible. Among them are these:

• Advertise the time and place of your sale, including
specific directions on how to get there. List a few eye-catching
items—baby furniture, children's clothing, and antiques if you

have them. Place a small classified ad in your local newspaper and post notices on the supermarket bulletin boards in your area. Then be prepared to have customers begin coming the night before, trying to get first crack at the choice items. Post directional signs at the major intersections near your home to intercept customers who may not have seen your ad.

• Mark the price on each item, and have some knowledgeable person determine what that price will be. It should be competitive with the going rates at garage sales in your area, but it is important that the pricer know the current retail value of the item. Juvenile clothing should be priced by a mother who knows the going prices in the stores, and so should toys. Someone who knows antiques should price them. Don't overprice and be prepared to bargain with the customers; for most of them, that's part of the fun.

• Don't be greedy. If someone makes an offer for an item which seems too low, but you sense that it is all she will pay, consider whether getting something isn't better than getting nothing and having to throw or give the item away at the end of the day. If you have children's clothing, price the name brands from the better stores at a higher price than the other brands, unless the clientele in your area isn't sophisticated enough to know the difference. Then, as the end of the sale nears, begin slashing prices on all items, particularly the large ones such as used appliances. It's better to get a small amount for them than to pay someone to cart them away. The perfect sale is one in which you maneuvered the pricing so skillfully that you got rid of everything for the maximum that your customers were willing to pay.

Clean all items and display them neatly so that no item will be overlooked. Don't assume that any item you have isn't worth including. There is a potential buyer for everything in this world, and sometimes the least likely items are the first to sell.

Have an understanding among the members that the merchandise was contributed for the good of the organization; if they want any of it they will have to pay the marked price, just like your clientele. Some organizational garage sales have been disasters because all of the best items were appropriated by the workers before the sale began. They felt they were entitled to the items as a reward for their work. Watch your customers, too, for some of them will not hesitate to walk away with something if you're not looking.

Garage sales are fun to do, and when they're over it is rewarding to know that your organization is several hundred dollars richer from selling items that your members were going to throw away!

Bazaars

Bazaars can be held at any time of the year but the most profitable are those conducted during the pre-Christmas season. At that time enterprising shoppers look for items to fill out their Christmas gift lists. Most of us struggle each year to find something special for a "hard to please" person on our list. Bazaars offer the opportunity to purchase exquisite hand-crafted items, some of them "one of a kind," at prices far below the value of the labor expended in making them.

An example of a successful bazaar is the one conducted in November of each year at the Highland Park (Illinois, Golf Club by the Arden Shore Association, which supports the Arden Shore Home for Boys. More than a dozen chapters of the association, located in different north suburban Chicago communities, join forces to present the bazaar, which consistently yields in excess of $30,000.

Work on the bazaar begins a year in advance, when each of the chapters appoints a bazaar chairman and committee chairmen to handle the myriad details associated with the event. Members determine the items they will produce for the bazaar. In many cases they organize into work groups that meet regularly at the home of individual members to work on the objects they will make. Everyone strives to come up with new ideas that will be more attractive than those offered by the members of other chapters, hoping to help their chapter produce the top results from the bazaar.

Booth decorations are prepared in advance so they need only to be installed on the day of the bazaar. Careful attention is given to pricing, so everything will be sold, but at the maximum yield. Workers are assigned to ensure that there will be enough on hand to take care of the customers and also provide security for the merchandise. An aggressive publicity campaign precedes the event, including the mailing of reminders to those who have attended in previous years.

Many groups have increased the profits from their bazaars by expanding them to include attractive features in addition to the handcrafted items for sale. These features include:

Entertainment for the children in the form of a miniature Christmas village, placed around a Christmas tree, with animated figures that add to the youngsters' delight

A baby-sitting service for mothers with small children, and shuttle bus service to a nearby parking lot when facilities at the bazaar locations are inadequate

A bake sale, featuring a variety of ethnic Christmas specialties

A Country Kitchen, to serve lunch and snacks

Entertainment by a musical group

A huge gingerbread house

An art booth featuring the work of local artists

Silent and oral auctions and raffles

A "slave market" in which services are auctioned; one group has persuaded the members of the local band to volunteer personal services, which are auctioned for a day

A prize drawing for which every guest may register

A very successful variation of the bazaar is the annual Christmas sale conducted in behalf of the Allendale School for Boys, which offers merchandise presented by exclusive shops located all over the country. The event is conducted in a motel situated in the heart of an affluent area; it attracts prosperous individuals who welcome the opportunity to expand their Yule shopping to exclusive emporia they otherwise could reach only by traveling to a dozen other states.

The sale, which lasts for a day, is preceded by a Patrons' Party the night before the event. Guests pay $20 a couple and are served cocktails and hors d'oeuvres. Their reward is first chance at the items displayed, and a chance to win a door prize donated by a local merchant. In 1977 the prize was a pair of diamond earrings. The guests that year had the opportunity to select Christmas gifts offered by Berrybridge, a garden accessory shop in St. Louis, Mo.; Chipp, Inc., a New York men's clothing shop; Gorsuch, Ltd., the ski apparel emporium in Vail, Colorado; Jean Gale's children's clothing shop in New York; Leap Frog, a New Vernon, N.J., gift shop; Lyon and Monograms, the Louisville, Kentucky, personalized gift shop; McArthur's Smokehouse, of Millerton, N.Y.; Papagallo Potpourri, the Darien, Connecticut, fashion shop; Past and Present, a Hobe Sound, Florida, gift shop; Sporting Spirit, of Ligonier, Pa.; T. Anthony, Ltd., the New York leather goods store; Tim's Originals, of Vero Beach, Florida, which sells needlepoint and paintings; and the Village Toy Shop, of Winnetka, Illinois.

Book sales

A book sale is another event that any group can conduct, offering donated merchandise and turning a certain profit. In any well-populated area there will be a horde of bibliophiles eager to attend and search for used books that interest them, many of them hoping to find a prized first edition.

The Vassar Club of Washington, D.C., supports scholarships for 16 students with the proceeds from their sale. The club collected 1800 *cartons* of books for its 1978 sale, the twenty-ninth one it has operated. The event runs for five days, and includes a silent auction of rare book and art print offerings.

The sale conducted by the Brandeis University Women's

Committee on Chicago's North Shore is billed as the largest in the world. The event is held in a large, striped tent that covers 17,000 square feet; in a typical year more than 200,000 books are offered for sale. The books are organized in 30 categories, and hardcover prices go as low as 40 cents.

The first Brandeis book sale in 1960 was conducted in a storefront with books sorted in member's basements. Today, volunteers pick up, sort, price, and store books throughout the year in a Highland Park warehouse. Admission to the sale, which runs for a week, is free except on opening night when a charge of $2.50 is made for those who want first chance to search for treasures on the one-third acre of tables. Typically, more than a thousand people are standing in line at noon for the 6 P.M. Saturday opening.

A special feature of the Brandeis sale is a closed bid auction of fine, rare books. Bids are time-stamped so that if there are equal high bids, the first bidder gets the book. The second weekend of the sale is bargain weekend, and prices are reduced. Books that remain at the end of the sale are not carried over, but donated to prisons, hospitals, and social service agencies.

Some groups provide coffee and food service for customers who may spend a day or more browsing through the books. Others offer baby-sitting services so that mothers can shop without being burdened by infants. Additional revenues can be generated through associated bake sales or craft boutiques.

Plant sales

If your membership includes amateur gardeners you can raise some money by conducting a plant sale in early spring, when the folks in your neighborhood are eagerly returning to their gardens. Your members can start annual plants in flats, and plant cuttings of their best house plants, which you will offer for sale. They can be repotted in almost any kind of container, but you can sell the plants for more money if you collect more attractive containers throughout the year, for repotting the better house plants that your members grow. Try to set up in an area with high density traffic, like a shopping center parking lot.

Specialized merchandise sales

Some groups conduct sales that are limited to a specific category of merchandise. The YMCA in Newark, Ohio, holds an annual quilt sale at which antique quilts are displayed and the work of contemporary quiltmakers sold. A $1 charge is made for admission to the three-day event.

Groups in many communities have capitalized on the increasing prices of athletic equipment by conducting sales of used bicycles, ice skates, and ski equipment. Members collect the used equipment from families whose children have moved on to larger sizes. These sales are socially useful, because they recycle the items, and offer bargains to parents at the same time.

Produce sales

If you have vegetable gardeners in your group you may be able to raise modest sums through one or more produce sales during the growing season. Most gardens produce more than their owners can use, and if you market the surplus at prices below those of the grocery store, you can readily convert vegetables into cash. An alternative, if you want to expand the charitable purposes of your group, is to collect the produce and offer it free to those in need. The East Aurora, New York, Nativity Lutheran Church does this by maintaining a surplus garden produce stand in its parking lot.

13

Food and drink

Luncheons, dinners, cocktail parties, and other events that offer food and drink are among the most popular and profitable fund raisers. Most of us enjoy eating out occasionally, and if good food and entertainment are offered at your dinner, many of those sympathetic to your cause will attend—if the price is not too much higher than what they would have spent at their favorite restaurant. If your dinner is held in a hotel or restaurant you get your profit from the markup you add to the cost of the meal. Better still, some organizations find an "angel" who is willing to underwrite the cost of the food; others serve dinners that have been prepared by the members of the group.

At the other end of the scale are the large, expensive dinners, usually held in the ballroom of a downtown hotel, where the tab is $50 a plate or more. They succeed by attracting guests who feel compelled to come because (a) the chairman of the dinner is a powerful person in the community whose prestige is riding on the outcome and they don't dare let him down; or (b) the dinner honors an individual who is prominent in the community and the guests feel that they must be seen at the event; or (c) the company that buys the table believes that, for public relations reasons, it must participate or be conspicuous by its absence. Many of the guests are there because they had a duty to help the company fill the table, and nobody has much fun. Nobody, that is, but the sponsors when they count the money they made.

Big dinners

The typical big city fund-raising dinner is conducted in a hotel ballroom, with tables of ten going for $500 and up. Few individual tickets are sold, most being sold as tables to corporations and financial institutions. The chairman will probably be the head of a large local corporation whose name at the bottom of the invitation virtually assures the sale of tables to his peers, bankers, suppliers, and others whose lives he can influence, or who owe him a quid pro quo. This "clout" effect is often multiplied by the announcement that another individual who also holds corporate or political power will be honored at the event.

The most difficult problem for the sponsors of this kind of dinner is finding a "wheel" who is willing to serve as chairman. More often than not this is accomplished by having this year's chairman recruit his successor, or by persuading the public relations department of a corporation that its image will be enhanced by having the president serve as chairman.

Once the chairman has been identified, a favorite strategy of many groups is to appoint a small army of vice chairmen—also business leaders—who agree to buy or be responsible for the sale of one or more tables. They accept this responsibility because they feel compelled to help the chairman make the dinner a success, or anticipate that they may need his help when they chair a fund raiser of their own. They also want their companies to benefit from the publicity that stems from their vice chairmanship of a worthy charitable event.

Many organizations that sponsor dinners of this sort recognize the disadvantages, the principal one being the diversion of many charitable dollars to the hotel in which the dinner is held. However, even though many companies are now refusing to participate for that reason, the dinners remain so profitable that most organizations continue to sponsor them because they extract money from many participants who otherwise would give nothing at all.

That the devices described here work is demonstrated by the annual "Golden Fellowship Dinner" conducted by the Chicago Urban League—the largest event of its kind in the city. They use this system, and in a typical year about 30 vice chairmen are involved, each responsible for a minimum of five tables at $1,500 each. In 1977 the dinner attracted 2,300 guests and raised nearly $450,000. The vast majority of the tickets were purchased or sold by vice chairmen.

If you try to conduct a dinner on this scale be sure to announce the date far in advance, and begin your ticket sales program well ahead of the event. Don't burden the guests with a long list of speakers; better still, don't have any. Try, instead, to persuade a popular singer or entertainer to donate his or her services to liven up the affair. One of the reasons the Chicago Urban League does so well is the reputation it has developed for staging an efficient affair, with no boring speeches, that offers first class entertainment and ends on time.

Some organizations pep up their dinners by conducting a raffle, holding an auction, or hiring a good band for an after-dinner dance. Others have enjoyed success by staging their dinner in an unusual place. The oldest and most successful zoo benefit in the nation is the annual Zoo-La-La conducted by the Women's Board of the Lincoln Park Zoological Society in Chicago. It's a black tie affair held under huge striped tents in the mall of the zoo. An annual benefit for the Gorton Community Center in Lake Forest, Illinois, is also held in a tent erected on the grounds of one of the large estates in the community. Guests are attracted by the novelty of the affair, and the opportunity to tour the mansion and the grounds.

Other groups excite interest by inviting their guests to appear in costumes of one sort or another. The Dix Hills, New Jersey, chapter of the National Asthma Center offers an "Oldies Night," highlighted by music and dress of bygone years. They serve hot smorgasbord and a five-course dinner, delight their guests, and make a lot of money.

Some groups have profited by tying in with another type of organization as sponsor of a fund-raising dinner. The Milwaukee, Wisconsin, chapter of the Muscular Dystrophy Association was the beneficiary of a $20,000 check raised at a testimonial dinner honoring the retiring president of Local 200 of the Teamsters Union, Roy Lane.

On a grander scale, "No Greater Love," a nonprofit organization founded by sports stars to aid the children of Vietnam war casualties, persuaded labor leader George Meany to allow it to conduct a fund raising birthday party in his honor. In addition to a host of sports personalities, the event attracted Vice President Walter Mondale, Secretary of Labor James Marshall, Secretary of Energy James Schlesinger, and so many guests that it took a half-ton of ice just to fill the water glasses!

If you can recruit a committee of prestigious local socialites to run it you can profit from a dinner which attracts guests who attend to maintain or enhance their social position. The dinner is an event at which they must "be seen." One such event, which got national press coverage, was a $50-a-head bash to raise money for the American syndicates competing in the America's Cup 12-meter yacht race. Jacqueline Onassis and her daughter, Caroline Kennedy, joined other celebrity guests on the lawn on Rosecliff Manor, in Newport, Rhode Island, where "The Great Gatsby" was filmed. They danced until the wee hours and when the sun came up had breakfast under pink tents.

Luncheons

Fund-raising luncheons appeal to two basic audiences—women with time on their hands who enjoy chatting with each other at social occasions, and businessmen who attend downtown luncheons because it is part of their job.

Typically, luncheons for women offer something to the guests besides food. This may be entertainment, an educational program, or even an attractive location that the guests would like to visit, such as lunch in the garden of a fashionable estate.

One group raised money for the local symphony association by conducting a luncheon that featured a recital by some of the symphony orchestra's talented members. Others have experienced success with celebrity guests, travelogues, book reviews, cooking demonstrations, flower arranging, style shows, and raffles or bid 'n buy auctions that offer guests the opportunity to go home with a prize. As with dinners, luncheons that are perceived to be socially prestigious are even more likely to succeed.

Most businessmen's luncheons feature a prominent speaker who will attract guests because of who he is or what he has to say. The guests buy tickets because they have to eat anyway, the price goes on their expense account, they have a chance to rub elbows with their peers or superiors—and they get a bonus if the speaker has something worthwhile to say. All of the other motivations described for dinners may also apply here.

Many organizations sponsor "report luncheons" to which their financial supporters are invited and asked to bring guests. These events are usually not fund raisers, per se, and the ticket price probably will do no more than cover the cost of the meal. Their value lies in reinforcing the interest of past donors, and soliciting new donors among the guests by displaying the accomplishments of the organization during the previous year.

Luncheons are also conducted by some groups as a means of reaching a large group of potential donors at one time, rather than making countless time-consuming individual calls. If you have an influential businessman as one of your present supporters, persuade him to host a luncheon for some of his peers. He picks up the tab, and representatives of your group make a presentation about its work and its benefits to society. The host then makes a closing pitch, pledge cards are distributed, and the guests are urged to make a commitment then and there. It's important to try to "close the sale" on the spot, because if the guests take the pledge cards away with them they probably will be pushed aside. Not all of the guests will be prepared to make a commitment at the luncheon, of course, so don't fail to follow up with personal attention.

Fashion shows

Fashion shows are usually presented as a feature of a luncheon or dinner, but some groups have successfully presented shows that stood on their own two feet. They can simply be displays of the current fashions, preferably from one of the better stores or the work of top designers, or you can sponsor a "trunk show" to which the leading couturiers bring a collection of the newest styles. The Heart Association of Lake County, Illinois, sponsored one of these events at Chicago's chic Ambassador West Hotel. Randazzo of Dallas shipped in a collection of its creations to be sold to the guests, with half the purchase price going to the Heart Association. The attraction of this event is the opportunity to buy a gown at the regular price, but actually get a discount because half the cost is tax deductible.

One of the advantages of first-class fashion shows, which feature top stores and prestige designers, is the society page news coverage they generate for your group. In a single column last year, one of Chicago's foremost society editors featured these events:

The first showing of Marshall Field & Company's fall collection, for the benefit of Lincoln Park Zoo

The Neiman-Marcus traveling show of new trends for the benefit of the Chicago Botanical Society

Carson, Pirie, Scott & Company's annual junior fashion show

A "fashion spectacular" presented by Lord & Taylor for the benefit of Delnor Hospital

"The Most Fashionable Night of the Year," featuring the collections of Ralph Lauren, Charles Suppon, Perry Ellis, Donna Karan and Louis Dell'Olio and Stephen Burrows, for the benefit of the Chicago International Film Festival

The Bonwit Teller fall fashion shows, held in a midtown location and featuring fashions for career women

Chicago was also the scene of a spectacular fashion show "first," sponsored by the Mental Health Association. The event, "NBC salutes Chic Chicago," was broadcast for 90 minutes on television station WMAQ. It featured an elaborate dinner in the ten-story Atrium atop the Apparel Center, featuring 70 of the top designers, and it was attended by the governor and mayor and their wives, and most of the city's social elite. The event, in addition to the television program, received major newspaper coverage and produced $24,000 for mental health.

Fashion shows do not have to be this elaborate, of course, nor need they feature the work of the most expensive designers. Many groups have conducted shows featuring the collections of local boutiques at which their members usually shop, or local designers not yet in the same league as Halston, Noriko, or Lauren. These luncheons can also include other features, such as the raffle of a designer gown.

Coffees and teas

Teas and coffees come in two varieties: some feature entertainment or other attractions; some are conducted simply as a means of reaching potential new members for the group. Popular features at the first variety are fashion shows, musical entertainment, and the demonstrations of various homemaking skills described in Chapter 18. You can levy a small admission charge for these events, the hostess supplies the coffee or tea, and the entertainment is also donated. Almost everything you take in is profit, since your only expense is the mailing of invitations to the event.

Membership coffees and teas are more serious business; your purpose is to do a "hard sell" on the guests whom you hope will support your cause or, better still, join your group. The invitation list may be limited to friends and neighbors of your members, personally invited by them, or it may be one that reaches a broader group of strangers whom you believe may have interest in your group. The first type of list will produce a fairly large response, but if you try a broadside mailing to strangers be prepared for a very low acceptance rate—probably no more than 10 percent, if that.

Guests at a membership tea should be exposed to a formal presentation of the purposes of your organization, a history of its past achievements, and a description of the benefits to the community that those accomplishments produced. Feature the aspects of your operations that bring pleasure to the members, and demonstrate that you are a warm and friendly group by asking each of your members to give personal attention to several of the guests. Make them like you and want to join your group so they can be with you again.

Cocktail parties

The cocktail party is similar to the coffee except that it is 80-proof. The addition of liquor to the equation may encourage your guests to open their wallets by placing them in a warmer, less cautious, more generous mood.

The party may be held in a restaurant or hotel, with a cash bar or an affluent sponsor—perhaps a corporation—to pick up the tab. It may also be a neighborhood affair, conducted in the home of a member or wealthy supporter who provides the liquor and hors d'oeuvres.

It is important that you find an excuse, however pallid, for the event. Your guests aren't apt to rush into a cocktail party if fund raising is the only purpose of the event. Wrap your party around some attraction that will be appealing to the prospective guests. Many will respond to the opportunity to meet a celebrity who, at the appropriate moment, will make a pitch for your group. It will also help if you can induce a prominent citizen to extend the invitations, introduce the celebrity guest, and, when the liquor has flowed long enough to stimulate a generous mood, "close the sale."

An alternative to the celebrity guest cocktail party is the event conducted in the home of a wealthy and socially prominent member or supporter. People will attend because they want to see how the other half lives, want the opportunity to meet the host and his wife, want exposure to other socially prominent guests they expect will be present, or simply because they look forward to describing the affair to their friends and neighbors over coffee the following morning.

Celebrity guests need not be limited to theatrical and political personalities. One group was successful with a party featuring a renowned chef who shared a few recipes with the guests. Another organization held a champagne party to honor Angelo Donghia, the internationally known furniture designer. Others have featured leading fashion designers, interior decorators, and leading specialists in arts and crafts.

Another option is the neighborhood cocktail party that capitalizes on the desire of most women to host better parties of their own. This affair could feature decorations by a leading florist or hors d'oeuvres prepared by a leading caterer. One group enjoyed success with a cocktail party to which each guest was asked to bring the recipe and samples of her own favorite hors d'oeuvre.

Rule No. 1 for cocktail parties: Be sure someone else pays for the booze!

Wine and cheese parties

Everyone seems to be drinking more wine these days, many of them self-consciously because they're embarrassed when they talk to the sommelier. Wine and cheese parties that offer wine-tasting have become popular because they add a feature that cocktail parties lack—the opportunity to learn more about wine.

To sponsor a wine and cheese party you need the cooperation of a local wine merchant, preferably one who is recognized for his expert knowledge of the grape. As a promotional effort for his business, he will donate several varieties of wine for tasting, and explain the distinctions and virtues of each of them to the guests.

You can profit directly from a wine and cheese party by levying an admission charge, or use it as a vehicle for soliciting larger donations from the guests.

Community dinners

Community dinners, and breakfasts and luncheons as well, are effective small-scale fund raisers for many organizations. They are most profitable if the food is prepared and donated by members, and you can hold them in a facility that doesn't charge any rent. They are most successful if they have a novel theme, offer unusual food, or offer convenience because they are associated with another event.

The daylong Fourth of July festivities in Lake Bluff, Illinois, get off to a healthy start at an "all you can eat" pancake breakfast in a village park. The meal is cooked by the members of the local Kiwanis Club and produces $400 to $500 for local charities every year.

A group in Milwaukee has capitalized on the Midwest taste for seafood by holding an annual clambake in the true New England style. Fresh oysters, clams, and barrels of seaweed are flown in from Massachusetts, along with a professional bake-master who prepares the clams. It is a very profitable event.

In Buffalo, New York, the Sandy Beach Yacht Club Women's Organization holds a Hawaiian luau. Guests are urged to wear Hawaiian costumes as they eat the traditional roast suckling pig and listen to dreamy Island tunes played on the electric guitar.

Try to pick a theme for your community dinner that will have special appeal to the potential guests in your community.

Ethnic dinners

Most of us enjoy sampling the traditional foods of other nationalities, as well as eating those of our own. Thus, ethnic dinners continue to be productive fund-raising events. They are appealing not only to the first generation immigrants in the community, but also to younger families that no longer cook the native dishes at home, but remember those delicious meals they ate at grandma's house.

Many churches in southern Wisconsin, which has a large Norwegian population, sponsor pre-Christmas lutfisk dinners. This is a traditional delicacy—fish that has been soaked in lye, rinsed and dried—that every good Norwegian associates with the Christmas holiday. It is something second and third generation Norwegians like to eat once a year, but probably no more often than that. The fish is cooked by members of the church, often the men's club, and served along with other delicacies and pastries that are Norse holiday traditions. Similar fund raisers are held in other ethnic communities; spaghetti, ravioli, or mostaccioli dinners in Italian neighborhoods; corned beef and cabbage for the Irish, and so on. Often traditional ethnic entertainment is provided.

Another option is the food fair at which a variety of ethnic foods are featured. A big one is sponsored in Buffalo, New York, by Neighborhood Housing Services, in cooperation with the Kensington Businessmen's Association. A street is closed to traffic for the Buffalo International Foods Fair, and booths offer a wide selection of international goodies, some prepared by individuals and some by restaurants that pay the sponsor for the privilege of offering their wares. In 1977 the fair featured native dishes of Mexico, the Philippines, China, France, Italy, Puerto Rico, plus Jewish food, and a selection of international vegetarian food. The food featured music, dancing, exhibitions, and an international fashion show.

Picnics

Picnics are appealing to parents whose children besiege them all summer with demands for "something to do." A family picnic can be fun, of course, but children enjoy them more when other kids are present and there are organized sports, games, and other events for their entertainment. Your group can make money by sponsoring a picnic at which it levies a small admission charge and supplies the food. Less profitable but also less work is the picnic to which guests bring their own baskets, but pay your group for the charcoal, drinks, and ice cream bars that it provides.

Ethnic picnics are also a favorite in many communities, usually sponsored by ethnic organizations that provide the food. Sts. Peter and Paul Greek Orthodox Church in Glenview, Illinois, has an annual Greek picnic featuring lemon-egg soup, lamb shishkebab, feta cheese, hot loukoumodes drenched in honey and sprinkled with cinnamon, ouzo, and chilled Greek wine. The members make and donate most of the food, and residents of the area have long since learned that you don't have to be Greek to enjoy it.

Added attractions for the guests at this picnic include a raffle and lessons in Greek dancing. Experts teach the kala-meatano, zembekeeko, and the hasapeeko to those who want to learn these dances; those who don't stand around shouting "Opa, opa!" and watch.

A bit of creativity can yield added attractions to lure guests to your picnic. A puppet show or pony rides for the kids will entice some families. One inspired political candidate in Seattle chartered a hot air balloon and sold rides to the guests.

Most picnics aren't big money raisers, but they are a good way for your members to raise small sums while getting to know each other better. The presence of the children adds a new dimension to your members' relationships.

Another option, if you have many affluent members or prospective guests, is the adult picnic that is really done in style. Most cities have caterers who will prepare fancy picnic baskets containing gourmet foods and wine. The prices range from $10 a basket into the hundreds of dollars. Kenessey Gourmets Internationale prepares a basket that costs $500 and serves eight. No potato chips and deviled eggs here: The basket contains eight one-pound lobsters, two pounds of beer-simmered shrimp, two whole roasted pheasants, Iranian caviar, pate, quiche, cheese, fruits, nuts and breads, six fifths of vintage wine, and a magnum of Dom Perignon.

One group on Long Island serves a basket of this quality at a $100-per-person picnic aboard the yacht of one of its members. No ants, and everyone has a colossal good time!

Potluck suppers

Most of us can't afford $100 picnics but have just as much fun at a potluck supper where we can sample a variety of foods cooked by others. Each guest brings a dish that will serve a dozen others. Your group levies a small charge for providing beverages and paper cups and plates. A little planning is necessary to make sure that you don't end up with 200 hot dishes, all macaroni and cheese. This is another good way to strengthen your group by bringing the members closer together. Some groups ask the guests to bring the recipe for the dishes that they provided, to form the basis for a cookbook that can be printed and sold.

Roasts

Although Dean Martin popularized them on television in recent years, these monstrosities have been around since the New York Friars Club roasted Will Rogers in 1904. Today, a few roasts are well-done, some are medium, but those at which the "roasters" are unfailingly humorous are exceedingly rare.

Nevertheless, many groups have enjoyed conspicuous financial success by roasting a well-known local celebrity. The drawing card is the celebrity and the other celebrities who put him on the pan. People come either as a tribute to the celebrity, out of curiosity about the celebrities who will be on the platform, or because they dislike the "roastee" with a passion, and hope to enjoy the insults that he will receive.

There has to be a better way to make a buck!

Other food events

The National Committee for the Prevention of Child Abuse persuaded a restaurateur to sponsor a 24-hour Eat-A-Thon which widened the eyes and the torsos of the gluttons in the community. Guests at the Town and Country restaurant in Chicago paid $5.75 for the privilege of stuffing themselves with all of the chicken, ribs, and omelets that they could eat in 24 hours. Hundreds of guests abused their stomachs to help fight child abuse.

Recipe exchanges are used by other organizations to raise money, mostly from their own members. Each guest brings a favorite recipe and a sample that the others present can taste. This is another method of securing recipes to be used in a cookbook that you can sell.

The American Cancer Society, in one city, was the beneficiary of a society fashion show staged at a continental break-fast in, of all places, a bustling local produce market.

The sale of food also provides a fund-raising opportunity. One group has an annual pizza sale which produces thousands of dollars. Orders are taken in advance, the pizzas are purchased from a local restaurant, and on the appointed day the buyers pick them up at a central location.

Finally, don't overlook the old standbys—barbecues, box socials, ice cream socials, and holiday cookie exchanges. All of them will swell your treasury by raising relatively small amounts, but if you do enough of them, the revenue can be an important source of income for your group.

14

Professional entertainment benefits

If you live in a large city with numerous theaters and concert halls where professional entertainment is offered, you have the opportunity to raise money by sponsoring a benefit performance that will have broad appeal to your members and their friends. Approach this type of fund raiser with caution, however, because you probably will be required to guarantee all or a large portion of the house; you can withstand losses if you commit your group to more tickets than it can sell.

The events you might sponsor include performances by road companies of Broadway shows, concerts of musical organizations that play everything from Bach to rock, movie premieres, celebrity and informational lectures, and trips to the circus or amusement park. If the play or concert is a sure sellout for its entire run, you may have to pay full box office price for the tickets you sell. If not, you can probably obtain a discounted group rate for the block of tickets you buy.

In either case, your profit comes from marking the tickets

up to the price you think the traffic will bear. Typically, groups that sponsor professional entertainment benefits will offer the best seats at prices ranging from $50 to $100, and price the less attractive seats down from there. The upper balcony will sell for only a modest increase over the normal price. This makes it possible for your supporters of almost any income level to participate in the event. Most of the more expensive tickets for these events are sold to corporations or other business organizations that have been persuaded to support your cause.

Be sure, before you undertake a theater benefit, to explore thoroughly the sales potential of the event. How many tickets can you sell to your own members? How many can they sell to others? How many can be sold to the public-at-large by advertising and promoting the event? The local promoters who bring these events to your city, and with whom you must negotiate the benefit, have had a great deal of experience with benefits and usually are able and willing to give you sound advice. Even though you have guaranteed the tickets, they have a stake in the success of the event. Their performers get annoyed if they find themselves playing to a half-filled house.

Plays and musicals

The safest way to sponsor a professional entertainment benefit, if the promoter will agree to it, is to have him hold the house for one evening and give you a few weeks to see how many seats you can sell. You will establish a cutoff date for your sales, after which the promoter will sell the remaining seats at the normal box office price.

Not all promoters will agree to this arrangement, however, because it reduces the time period during which they can try to sell out the house. Consequently, you may have to guarantee to purchase a block of tickets, or the entire house, and pay for them whether you can sell them or not.

Some groups induce customers to purchase the higher priced tickets by arranging a reception for the star or cast.

Other groups in smaller cities where live entertainment is scarce have prospered by sponsoring one- or two-night stands featuring road companies of Broadway shows. Again, this requires a substantial guarantee, and you should not undertake such an event without getting sound professional advice. You may also find your choices limited by the adequacy of the theatrical facilities in your community. You will probably be limited to plays rather than musicals, which require elaborate lighting and stage equipment.

Concerts

Professional concerts may also be sources of funds if you sponsor a benefit similar to those described for theatrical events. You can sponsor benefit performances of name stars being presented by professional promoters, concerts by the local symphony or other local professional musical groups, or you can engage a professional singer or musical group. If you're lucky you may be able to exploit your nonprofit purposes and persuade the entertainer to donate his services or provide them at less than his usual fee.

Even if you are sponsoring the event yourself, however, it is wise to work with a professional theatrical promoter in staging the event. It will probably cost you a fee or a commission, but consider that as insurance against a disastrous result.

Obviously, you will want to sponsor the kind of music that has the greatest appeal in your community. In recent years, however, rock concerts by the more popular groups have been almost certain winners in almost any locale. You will draw the young audience in your own community, plus fans who follow the itinerary of the most popular rock bands, traveling hundreds of miles to hear them when they are in their area.

Movie premieres

If a major motion picture is filmed in your locality, try to arrange with the producer to present a benefit premiere of the film for your group. Producers often agree because it is good promotion for their film. It is also a sure winner for you. Some of the major studios also schedule local premieres of their films in many cities across the country and are sometimes willing to present them as benefit events. People attend premieres, paying substantially more to see the film than if they waited a few days, because of the glamor they see in premiere events. To make it work well, however, you must have a commitment from the producer, star, and some of the principal cast members to attend the event.

In 1977 when Robert Altman was looking for a mansion in which to film "The Wedding," he approached Mrs. Lester Armour, of the meat-packing family, and asked if he could use her home in Lake Bluff. The film had an outstanding cast, headed by Carol Burnett, Lillian Gish, and Howard Duff.

Mrs. Armour has been interested in the work of the Rehabilitation Institute of Chicago. She told Altman he could use her home if (1) he donated $40,000 to the Institute, and (2) he scheduled the premiere performance in Chicago as a benefit for the Institute. He agreed to both conditions, and the film was made.

When the film was released in April, 1978, the Women's Board of the Rehabilitation Institute capitalized fully on the opportunity. They created a package that included "Dinner with the Stars," at the Casino, the film showing, and a subsequent cast party at the Drake Hotel. The package sold for $150 per person and so many orders were received that hundreds of checks had to be returned. Others guests were permitted to attend the theater showing and the cast party for $45, or the theater alone for $15.

Opportunities like this don't appear very often, but it is wise to keep track of film production activities in your locality, because the same thing could happen to you.

On a smaller scale, you can also consider sponsoring films that can be rented from distributing companies, or obtained from various business organizations and professional societies.

Your telephone directory will help you to identify distributors, and the people who publish it—the Bell System companies—will be happy to send you a catalog of films in their library. You may present films independently, or use them as the entertainment feature for a luncheon, dinner, or other fund-raising event.

Celebrity lectures

At any given time there are dozens of celebrities whom many people would like to see and hear. They include political leaders, best-selling authors, and even individuals who are notorious for their role in some current event, *i.e.* Watergate's John Dean. Most of them are willing to speak and, in fact, for many of them this is a major source of income. Some of them, particularly the politicians, will address charitable organizations without demanding a fee.

Some groups present individual lectures and others arrange a lecture series throughout the year. These can be quite profitable but, like other forms of professional entertainment, they involve a degree of risk. Don't undertake one unless you are certain that your receipts will exceed the amount of the lecture fee.

Amateur entertainment

Depending upon the talent available within your group, and how your community reacts to them, don't overlook the possibility of sponsoring amateur events. Even though they have been around for a long time, organizations are still experiencing success with all of these: amateur nights, magic shows, amateur plays, musical revues, minstrel shows, variety and vaudeville shows, and performances by organized local choral groups, orchestras, and bands. None of these events is likely to produce huge sums, but they will supplement the funds you raise from other events. They also teach your members to work together and can be a lot of fun.

Small sums can also be raised by talented members who present book reviews or poetry readings. The Langston Hughes Cultural Arts Center in Seattle combined music and poetry that had appeal to two special groups when it presented a program of Native American music and women's poetry. They provided a baby-sitting service and charged two dollars.

15

Holiday events

Fund raisers associated with holidays have something special going for them—the warm reception they get because everyone is in an especially good mood. This is most evident during the Christmas holidays when the spirit of giving fills the air. Plan at least one event that capitalizes on the spirit of the holidays.

This, incidentally, applies to your fund-raising solicitations, as well. The weeks preceding Christmas are the best time to solicit individual, corporate, and foundation donors for contributions to your group. This is true not only because you are apt to find everyone in a more generous frame of mind, but for three other reasons. First, many individuals are reviewing their income tax situation and may find it prudent to make some additional charitable contributions. Second, many foundations budget a sum for undesignated purposes and find, as December 31 approaches, that they have remaining funds. You may be able to persuade them to give some of this money to your group. Third, this is the period during which many foundations are drawing up their budgets for the coming year. While your solicitation may not produce a gift immediately, it may prompt the foundation to include your organization in its budget for the following year.

Christmas

Most of the events already discussed will enjoy even greater success if they are scheduled during the Christmas holidays and built around a Christmas theme. Your luncheon or dinner might feature fashions for the holidays, for example. One group that conducts a Christmas fashion show attracts additional guests to it's luncheon by offering as a door prize a $1,000 Christmas shopping spree. The gift certificates are donated by several local merchants. Demonstrations also take on added interest if they are related to a holiday. A program on Christmas flower arrangements, gift wrapping, or holiday cooking is always appealing to persons looking for fresh ideas. Another group's luncheon features Christmas in art and music; an art historian discusses how artists since the birth of Christ have interpreted the Christmas story. Reproductions of the artists' work are displayed and an ensemble plays the Christmas songs of various lands.

The Christmas season is the best time for bazaars, as shoppers hunt for unusual gifts or novel, handmade decorations for their homes or Christmas trees. One group combines a housewalk with its bazaar, and features one room on the tour that typifies an "old fashioned Christmas." It is furnished in the Victorian manner, and brightened with antique Yule decorations from bygone years. The room has great appeal to nostalgia buffs and antique collectors.

Christmas is for children, so you can also make money with events planned especially for them. A favorite is "Luncheon with Santa," a hot dog and soda pop feast that includes entertainment and a visit from Santa Claus. Each child receives a small gift. Although the event is for children, the attendance is increased because most of the children are accompanied by one or both parents.

Ethnic dinners also take on an added meaning at Christmastime, because almost all nationalities have developed a host of special dishes and pastries that are traditional at this time of the year. A Christmas party with traditional ethnic music or dancing will provide an attractive lure.

Some groups, aware of the shopping difficulties experienced by mothers with infant children, earn a modest sum by providing baby-sitting services during the holidays. Another group conceived the novel idea of placing a huge Christmas card in the window of a small town store. For a donation, residents could wish their friends and neighbors a "Merry Christmas" by adding their names to the card.

The Latin School, a nonprofit private elementary and high school in Chicago, derives financial support from a "Live and Learn" adult education series, scheduled for six consecutive weeks beginning in early October. Included are classes that teach gift wrapping, how to make candy food fantasies like marzipan, how to build a gingerbread house, the art of quilling snowflake ornaments, paper sculpture, and Christmas table decoration. They charge $40 for the six-lesson course.

Finally, don't overlook the opportunity to sell things that most people buy at Christmastime. There are the obvious ones, like Christmas trees, wreaths, mistletoe, fruitcake, pine and holly boughs, Christmas cards and stationery. But you can also profit from the sale of various types of Christmas gift items, such as fruit baskets, boxes of citrus fruit that are shipped directly to the recipient, and assortments of cheese, candied fruit, and nuts. The popularity of the Mexican custom of lighting luminaria at Christmastime led one group to sell kits for this purpose. They provide everything you need to assemble those sand-filled paper bags containing candles that glow along your driveway at Christmastime.

In Chicago, an imaginative group of supporters of Children's Memorial Hospital multiplied the returns from their

Christmas-tree sale by asking prominent Chicagoans to decorate them first. Fully-decorated "ArtisTrees" were provided by many socialites, including the state's "first lady," Jayne Thompson, and the wife of Chicago Blackhawks owner Arthur M. Wirtz, Jr. They sold for handsome prices.

New Year's Eve

The urge that most of us have to celebrate the advent of the New Year is one on which you can capitalize to divert some dollars from the cash registers of the local nightclubs into the coffers of your own organization. Plan a party at the home of one of your members or hire a band and rent or borrow a hall and create a nightclub of your own. You can charge a flat fee to cover the costs of the food, entertainment, and liquor, or charge a smaller fee and run a cash bar that serves the liquor. The abstainers in your group will favor the second option. Don't forget to supply the hats and horns to make your guests feel like kids again when midnight arrives. A do-it-yourself New Year's Eve party will be fun for the guests and for those who plan it, particularly those who enjoy expressing themselves in the decorating to create the nightclub atmosphere.

Halloween

The biggest fund raiser on Halloween is, of course, the "trick or treat" collection made for UNICEF by children throughout the United States. In a typical year they raise three million dollars to purchase food, health, and educational supplies for less fortunate children in developing nations.

You'll have to settle for less than that, but there are other profitable options your group can exploit to capitalize on this occasion. A perennial favorite with many organizations is the haunted house, which the children of the community can visit and pay for the privilege of being scared out of their wits. Your members will enjoy it too, because it provides another outlet for their creative instincts.

Most organizations that develop haunted houses find an old, vacant property that they can decorate and equip. It is amazing what a spooky atmosphere can be created with simple scenery, ingenious lighting, and recorded sound effects. If you can't find a house to work with, the same can be achieved within a large room in a local school or community center.

Halloween luncheons, dinners, and dances are other options. You can also make money by setting up shop in a high traffic area and having a pumpkin and cider sale.

Thanksgiving

Think turkey and cranberries and pumpkin pie and apply them to any of the food events already mentioned. Some groups sell cranberries prior to this holiday; turkey raffles are conducted by others. It's also a good season for a Turkey Shoot.

Independence Day

The Fourth of July is a great day for a picnic or carnival, or a local festival complete with parade. Because most states have now outlawed fireworks except in professional hands, you might also consider sponsoring a fireworks display. Obtain permission to use a stadium or large, open park area, and engage one of the commercial fireworks companies to·present the display for you. Be sure you have adequate insurance coverage, because fireworks are inherently dangerous and accidents do happen. Try to select a site that has ample parking, and if not, arrange for shuttle bus service tò nearby parking lots. Charge a small fare to cover the cost of the buses. You make your profit from a small general admission charge. Some groups make no charge for general admission, but provide reserved seating at a higher fee. Set up some concession stands which will be eagerly patronized by all of the kids at the event.

An Exchange club in the East sponsored a fireworks display in the city stadium that attracted more than 100,000 guests. Most parents with small children are compelled to visit some local fireworks display, and for many of them the crowds and traffic are an ordeal they would rather avoid. The easier your display is to get to and get out of the greater your chances are of attracting a substantial crowd. If you do, the event will grow, from word-of-mouth advertising, year after year.

Labor Day

This holiday, the last long summer holiday weekend, is another great day for a picnic or parade, or for a professional carnival. But be careful: Your market may be smaller than you think because so many families will be taking advantage of the last opportunity to get out of town.

Athletic events

The Kentucky Derby isn't a national holiday but it might as well be. The same goes for the Rose Bowl and all the other "bowl" games, the professional Superbowl, the Indianapolis 500, and a few other major athletic and sports spectaculars. Many groups plan parties associated with these events.

16

Athletic, sports events

Sponsorship of athletic tournaments and events provides substantial revenue for hundreds of nonprofit groups. Everyone is familiar with the larger charitable events that even attract national television coverage because of the celebrities involved in them. The Bing Crosby Golf Classic is a dramatic example. You probably won't be able to persuade ex-President Ford to be a spectator at your tournament, but it is possible to conduct these events on a local basis with excellent results.

Organizations throughout the nation benefit from pro-am golf and tennis tournaments, featuring national or local professionals or celebrities who play a round with the guests. Some groups sponsor local amateurs against representatives from golf and tennis clubs in other cities.

Phyllis Diller came up with a new twist in charity tennis tournaments in 1978 when she sponsored a "comedy tennis classic" in Houston, Texas, Jonathan Winters, Woody Allen, Chevy Chase, and a dozen other comics competed. The spectators agree that most of the tennis was funnier than the repartee, but a nonprofit civic theater group was richer when it was over.

Some organizations sponsor baseball or softball teams or leagues, both amateur and semiprofessional, and profit from admission fees and refreshments sold at the games. Bizarre one-shot events like donkey softball, old-timers' baseball, and performances by groups like the Harlem Globetrotters basketball team, competing against local talent, also draw crowds.

If your city is basketball or hockey happy, you might sponsor an exhibition of one of these. In other cities a bowling tournament, skiing competition, or swimming meet might be the thing. Turkey Shoots go over big in some communities, and you don't have to live in cowboy country to make money with a first-class professional rodeo. Also, don't forget Road Rallies, which make money and are fun for your members and guests. Or, forget about horsepower and attract some real horses to your horse show.

Remember, always, that any time you can lure a celebrity to participate you'll increase the gate at your event. In 1978 the Cape Cod Charity Horse Show in Mashpee, Massachusetts, featured Linda Blair, the star of "The Exorcist," as one of the riders. She won the blue ribbon in the large junior hunter's class, and the proceeds helped local charities exorcise some of their obligations.

Another form of athletic event is one that generates publicity by pitting bizarre opponents against each other. An example is the annual basketball game in Washington, D.C., conducted for the benefit of the Metropolitan Police Boys Clubs. It attracts attention and reinforces the charitable purpose of the game by matching District of Columbia police officers against inmates of the Lorton, Maryland, reformatory.

Some organizations have performed a public service and produced income for themselves by developing winter sports facilities in their communities. It isn't terribly costly to construct a skating rink, toboggan slide, or simple ski run that youngsters in your community will cheerfully pay a small fee to enjoy.

Finally, let's not forget one that isn't exactly athletic, but fits here as well as anywhere else. It's the celebrity "dunk tank" dreamed up by the Muscular Dystrophy group in Seattle, Washington. They set up a carnival dunk tank in the Seattle Center's Plaza of States and persuaded local celebrities to sit on the stool. Participants pay for the privilege of throwing a baseball to try to dump them in the water.

Imagine what one of those could earn if the victim were Howard Cosell!

17

Services, training, education

Three characteristics of contemporary society can be exploited to create this category of fund-raising activities. One is the difficulty many families experience in trying to find workers willing to perform needed services around their houses. The second is the growing emphasis on "do-it-yourself" projects. The third is the growing interest in self-improvement, evidenced by the enormous sales of "how to" books.

The service category offers a variety of opportunities. You can conduct a one-shot event, such as a weekend car wash in a convenient parking lot. If you can recruit the manpower, you can offer a single service, such as yard work and snow shoveling on a year-round basis. Or you can operate a mini-employment agency providing a variety of services.

Services you can provide

Your problem is finding someone to do other people's work

149

for them. If you plan something as simple as a weekend car wash, the work can be done by your own members, or by members of a local youth group that you recruit to help you as one of their community service projects. The year-round operations, however, will require that you recruit individuals who actually become your employees. Your profit will come from a markup on the hourly charge for their services or, to put it another way, a commission on what they receive for their services. A variation that some groups have used successfully is a summer employment service utilizing out-of-school youth. This offers several benefits. It gives young people something constructive to do during the summer months, and money they can use when go back to school. Meanwhile, residents of your community are relieved of the need to do their own lawn mowing, fix-up painting, and other arduous summer chores.

An example of a successful summer youth employment is that conducted by Job Opportunity for Youth (JOY) in Lake Forest and Lake Bluff, Illinois. The service has been operated for nearly a decade, with young people doing lawn work, cleaning basements, washing windows, baby-sitting, cleaning swimming pools, caring for pets, weeding gardens, doing housework, cleaning gutters, serving at parties, and any other job that doesn't require a high level of skill. Young people are also employed to answer the telephone and assign workers to the job orders received. Customers of the service buy coupon books with which they compensate the workers who, in turn, redeem the coupons they earn for cash.

The same principle can be applied to a year-round employment agency, using adult workers as well as youngsters, and perhaps offering services such as house painting, which require a higher level of skill. In most communities there are adult residents, such as housewives and retired persons, who would like to earn some money but are unwilling or unable to work full-time. Another source of help is among workers in seasonal occupations who want something to do when they are laid off from their regular jobs. Since most of your employment agency's requests will be for one-shot or part-time help, workers looking for part-time jobs make an ideal fit.

A variation utilized by one nonprofit group is a referral service for "summer girls" or mother's helpers, desired by many families with young children during the months when there is no school. They advertise for girls in nearby small town newspapers, and in the local high schools, and then match the applicants with job orders from families in the community.

Other services that have been offered successfully by charitable organizations include a permanent baby-sitting facility in a suburban shopping plaza, used by mothers who don't want to be burdened with kids while they shop; mobile food services that supply sandwiches and lunches at auctions and other events of long duration and substantial crowds; and envelope addressing services for commercial organizations that do a lot of advertising by direct mail. One chapter of the Order of the Eastern Star sponsors an annual pillow-cleaning service, with a team of workers who recover each pillow with new ticking in a choice of fabrics and colors. Many groups have sponsored Cut-A-Thons in cooperation with local beauty salons. The salon, as a means of introducing its services to a new group of potential customers, provides free haircuts; the charitable group receives a donation from each lady who is shorn.

The First Presbyterian Church of Lake Forest, Illinois, sponsor of the highly successful bazaar described previously, employed an imaginative variation of personal service fund raising in order to send its choir on a "Highland Sing" in Scotland. Members of the congregation were persuaded to donate various services, craft items, and other merchandise on which participants could bid by mail.

A fascinating array of services were offered. One couple, for $60, offered to baby-sit two children in their home for a weekend. Other services included addressing Christmas cards, wrapping Christmas presents, driveway snowplowing, gutter cleaning, ironing, and a limousine service provided by a member with a chauffeur-driven Cadillac. Lessons were offered in tennis, bridge, skiing, voice, and on a number of muscial instruments. Season-ticket holders for various musical and athletic organizations offered their tickets for specific dates. Every conceivable craft, including a handmade grandfather clock, was represented, as well as a variety of merchandise. The most unusual item was presented like this:

"HORSE MANURE FOR YOUR GARDEN!: Definitely an unusual Christmas gift! Put your garden to bed now under a blanket of it, or take an IOU for next spring. You bag it— $15.00+ per load."

Do-it-yourself training programs

The opportunities to offer training in various fields is limited only by your own imagination and ingenuity. Programs may offer instruction in arts and crafts, cooking, decorating, gardening, and any other human activity you can name. They can be one-shot affairs, or a series of demonstrations presented regularly over a period of weeks or months. Here is a sampling of instructional programs already conducted successfully by nonprofit groups:

Microwave cooking
Cuisinart cooking
Crepemaking
Bagel making
Ice cream concoctions (pre-
  sented by Baskin-Robbins)
Understanding wine
Entertaining etiquette
Home entertainment ideas

Children's party ideas
Flower arranging
Interior decorating
Make your own clothes
Knitting
Embroidery
Macrame
Making ribbon pillows
Drying garden and roadside
    flowers
Fabric flowers
Origami
Weaving
Spinning
Chair caning
Sand art
Glassblowing
Japanese brush painting
Growing bonsai trees
Care of house plants
Outdoor gardening
Transcendental meditation
    and yoga
Brass rubbing
Self-defense—Karate, judo, ai-
    kido, and kendo
Artificial respiration and the
    Heimlich maneuver
How to use cosmetics
Identifying genuine antiques
Baby-sitter clinic

Commercial organizations will provide expert instructors in some of these skills without charge to your group. Others can be conducted with experts who are on the faculties of local colleges and universities. Still others may be presented by individuals in your community who have developed a high level of skill in one speciality or another. The important thing is to maximize your profit by finding speakers who won't charge for their services.

Self-improvement courses

Depending upon the complexity of the subject, self-improvement courses may be presented as a single lecture or as a series presented back-to-back or over a period of time. They can deal with almost any aspect of personal concerns—physical or emotional well-being, child-rearing, marital relationships, family finances, investments, career counseling, and so on.

The Lake-Cook YWCA in Highland Park, Illinois, presents an annual program, "How to Survive in College," for young people who have just graduated from high school and will enter college in the fall. A panel of college students discusses details that concern prospective students such as what to take to college, what kind of clothes to buy, what the student's personal financial needs will be, course selection, how to study, the pros and cons of fraternities and sororities, and even how to behave at a party.

Another group sponsored a program of travel tips for couples about to embark on their first trip abroad. It dealt with all of the small details that concern first-time overseas travelers—language problems, tipping, transportation, and so on. Lectures that appeal to the emerging woman are also popular these days. Many women want and need to know more about investments, estate planning, and career opportunities.

The important consideration in planning self-improvement presentations is to study the interests of large groups of persons in your community and plan events that meet their needs and desires. Here are some ideas that have been successfully used by other groups:

Investments for women
Career opportunities for women
Selling your home
Wills and estate planning
Is your insurance adequate?
Diets and health
Is your child hyperactive?
How to relate to teenagers
Is your marriage in trouble?
Collecting art and antiques for profit
Effective public speaking
How to handle boredom and depression

All of the fund-raising ideas in this chapter will raise money, but they have another virtue in common. Each of them offers something more than entertainment. They provide needed services to your community.

18

Potpourri

After you have fed the residents of your community all they care to eat, sold them all the antiques and hand-me-downs they want to buy, provided all the services they can use, exhausted possibilities to entertain them, and filled their heads with everything they want to learn, is there anything else you can do to persuade them to part with some of their money? Yes, indeed. Here are some more ideas for you to consider that have worked for other groups:

Product sales

Many groups have discovered that the sale of products by their members is one of the most effective ways to raise money. It is a method that reaches people who may never give to charity, but who are willing to buy a product that they use regularly at a price reasonably comparable to what they would normally expect to pay. Candy sales are good because the product is instantly consumable; this is attractive to buyers whose sweet tooth reacts upon seeing the candy in the salesperson's hand.

Some measure of the popularity of sales of candy, peanuts, pretzels, and other edibles can be gleaned from studying the volume of business done by firms that specialize in the sale of these items to charitable organizations.

Mrs. Sittler's Candies, Cicero, Illinois, sells 125,000 pounds of chocolate covered candies and peanut brittle every year. It is worth $375,000, and is sold primarily by Scout, school, and Little League groups.

Kathryn Beich Fund-Raising Candies in Forest Park, Illinois, sells 40,000 pounds of candy a week—$2 million worth a year—mostly to school groups.

Old Fashioned Candies in Berwyn, Illinois, annually sells 5,000 boxes of taffy apples at $4.20 per box, 5,000 pounds of peanut brittle at $1.15 per pound, and 1,000 pounds of chocolate and nut candies at $4.70 a box. School groups are its primary customers.

Miss Dolly Madison, in Hammond, Indiana, sells 750,000 pounds of candy worth $2 million in Chicago and its suburbs each year.

Snack foods are also attractive to buyers, and even more so to the groups that sell them, because most of them are marked up 100 percent. The 1978 Kiwanis Kid's Day Peanut Sale in Chicago sold more than seven million bags of peanuts supplied by the Ace Pecan Co., of Elk Grove Village, Illinois. Suburban buyers consumed 75,000 pizzas prepared for charitable groups by Lorenzo's Frozen Foods, Ltd., of Westchester, Illinois. Their appetites unsatisfied, they also consumed nearly 100,000 pounds of pretzels supplied by the International Pretzel Company of Calumet City, Indiana, and Fritz Soft Pretzel, of Barrington, Illinois. Iroquis Popcorn in Elk Grove Village sold 100,000 pounds of unpopped corn to fund-raising groups, along with an avalanche of snow cones, cotton candy, and candy apples.

Many youth groups sell candy and other foods door-to-door, or in supermarket parking lots, then deliver the merchandise on the spot. Others, like the Girl Scouts with their annual cookie sale, take advance orders from customers, order the required amount of merchandise, and deliver it at a later date.

You can sell almost anything to make money for your group if most people use it and it is moderately priced. An organization in the West raised $700 selling action labels—peel-off labels that contain various kinds of emergency instructions, telephone numbers, and other warnings and reminders. The profit on these items is 100 percent. Many Parent-Teacher Associations raise substantial sums by selling warmup suits, sweatshirts, T-shirts, and even patches bearing the school name. Other groups have capitalized on the T-shirt craze by buying the equipment used to imprint them with individual names or other slogans and designs.

Other relatively inexpensive equipment is available for personalizing various items. You can get simple metal engraving equipment to personalize Christmas ornaments. A $34.95 kit is available with which you can produce personalized badges. They sell for a dollar and the materials cost ten cents. Still another device can be obtained with which you can imprint individual names on ordinary lead pencils, an attractive item to parents whose children are always losing their pencils at school.

Some groups—the Girl Scouts among them—print attractive calendars which they sell year after year. Others, including the Junior League, sell attractive personalized stationery. One Exchange Club made $1,400 selling personalized paper napkins. Other groups have profited from the sale of gift wrap packages and assortments of birthday and other cards.

The list of products that have been sold successfully is almost endless, but it also includes American flags, brooms, bug bombs, charcoal, flowers, first aid kits, lawn products, light bulbs, magazine subscriptions, needle threaders, soap, toothbrushes (one group raises $10,000 a year from these), citrus fruit, and pecans. Creative groups come up with new ideas every year.

Special publications

Many groups profit from the sale of "ad books" that are distributed to their members and others in the community. In most cases the principal income comes from the sale of advertising to local merchants, but some of these publications are of sufficient interest that people will buy them for the information they contain. Examples of the latter include local histories, usually published in association with a local anniversary celebration; entertainment guides; city maps, in communities where none is available through service stations or other outlets; local telephone directories covering small suburbs of cities where all the metropolitan numbers are included in one large book; and books of helpful household hints.

Cookbooks offer a special opportunity to women's organizations. Some merely contain a variety of favorite recipes supplied by members of the organization. Others deal with specialized forms of cooking; microwave cookbooks and Cuisinart cookbooks are currently popular. Still other groups gather the favorite recipes of national or local celebrities and incorporate them into a book. The organizations that publish them profit from the sale of the books and from paid advertising placed in the book by local merchants.

Running your own business

Many organizations that conduct annual rummage sales have discovered that they can profit throughout the year by operating thrift shops which sell used clothing, appliances, radio and television sets, toys, baby equipment, furniture, and other items. These stores convert donated merchandise into cash, and at the same time provide a valuable service to economically deprived families who could not afford to buy new merchandise of comparable quality in the stores. Rummage sale merchandise that is received throughout the year is carefully sorted and the better items are placed in the thrift shop for immediate sale. The remainder is stored until the rummage sale occurs. If you undertake this kind of operation you will, of course, need an ample supply of willing volunteers to man the store.

Other groups maintain gift shops that stock handmade craft items made by their members. The handmade merchandise is supplemented with manufactured gift items that have customer appeal. Many women will patronize these shops because they can satisfy their need for gift items while helping to sustain an organization whose cause they favor. In some cases, these shops are located in hospitals, in which case they sell candy and flowers, as well. They are a convenience for those who need gifts or flowers for friends and relatives who are patients in the hospital. Other groups have arranged with the management of hospitals to operate small cafés that offer coffee and limited food service to hospital visitors.

Discount tie-ins

The supermarkets in some cities, eager to lure new customers to their stores, are amenable to staging days on which a percentage of their proceeds goes to charitable groups. In the typical arrangement, a notice is posted that on X day 5 percent of the price paid for merchandise purchased at the store will be donated to a specific charity upon presentation of the cash register receipts. Your organization is expected to encourage its members and friends to shop at the store and supply you with the receipts. The success of this enterprise will be determined by the zeal with which you make sure that as many shoppers as possible save and give you their receipts.

A variation of this system is employed by the Jewel Food

supermarkets in the Midwest. They supply "Shop and Share" coupons to charitable organizations for distribution to their members. Customers, after they have paid for their merchandise, turn in the shop and share coupon, along with their cash register receipt, at the service desk. The store accumulates all of the receipts and sends the organization a check for 5 percent of the total amount purchased.

Other discount arrangements include those, usually arranged with apparel stores, in which the store supplies your organization with coupons good for a 20 percent discount on all merchandise sold to the holder. Your members and others to whom you distribute the discount coupons are encouraged to shop in the store to secure the discount. The store, in turn, gives your organization an additional 10 percent of the amount sold to discount coupon holders.

Some groups have made substantial sums by negotiating with numerous merchants, restaurants, nightclubs, and theaters in the community for discount arrangements. Discount coupon books are then sold to thrifty customers. The coupon book may provide discounts totaling $500 to holders who use them all. You sell the book for $10. Many merchants are happy to cooperate in these ventures because the coupons introduce new customers to their enterprises.

Salvage

The environmental movement has spurred interest in recycling and improved the prospects for success of organizations willing to undertake the salvage of old newspapers, aluminum cans, and other reusable items. The Old Guard, a senior citizen group in Bricktown, New Jersey, has provided a dozen scholarships to local youth by recycling newspapers. The women of St. Thomas Moore Church, in Brooklyn, Ohio, repaved the church parking lot the same way.

The average American reads about 100 pounds of newspapers a year, and barely 25 percent of them are recycled, so there is a profitable opportunity for any group to try to collect the 75 percent that is still going to waste. If you want to find out how to do it write to the American Paper Institute, Inc., Paper Stock Conservation Committee, 260 Madison Avenue, New York, N.Y. 10016, for their booklet, "How to Recycle Waste Paper."

The students at Manley High School in Chicago help clean up their neighborhood and earn money to buy extra equipment for shop classes by recycling used aluminum beverage cans. In the spring of 1978, when aluminum was selling for 20 cents a pound, the Manley kids collected enough cans to earn $290. It takes 16 to 20 cans to make a pound.

Said Joe Mazanek, one of the school's shop teachers: "The students love it. It's really a competition out there. You can pick up one hundred cans in a block on Monday morning, but by Friday you've got to pull teeth to find any cans in our area.

"The students are really doing four things in this project. They're making money to supplement the shop class budget. They're cleaning up the neighborhood. They're helping to conserve resources and energy. And they're having a lot of fun."

Direct mail and door-to-door solicitation

Mass direct mail solicitation is a high cost, low yield method of fund raising that is not recommended for any but the largest national organizations. The exception might be a mailing by your organization to a highly selective and unusually promising list.

Door-to-door solicitations, on the other hand, can be the most productive way to raise money, but with a very important caveat. You must have a membership that is willing to do this hard and often unpleasant work, or the capacity to recruit volunteers who will do it for you. It is not the kind of fund raising that many of us consider fun.

Miscellaneous

Some organizations have developed innovative fund-raising methods that fit no particular category, but are profitable nonetheless.

Sponsors of commercial entertainment events are always looking for new ways to promote their enterprise. The Mental Health Association of Lake County capitalized on this by making an ingenious arrangement with King Richard's Faire, a month-long festival held each year in southern Wisconsin: Family passes were printed and placed in banks and other prominent places for use by guests who attended the fair. Upon presentation of the pass at the ticket window the association received $1 for each adult ticket purchased. The customer got nothing extra but the satisfaction of helping a charitable cause, but the association was enriched, and the fair exposed to a lot of new customers.

When B. Dalton Booksellers opened a new store in Chicago it gave a champagne party to celebrate the event. Charlton Heston, William Simon, and other authors were present as special guests. To swell the attendance, the store worked out an arrangement to extend invitations to supporters of Children's Memorial Hospital, which received all of the store's book sale proceeds on the day of the event.

Grove School, an institution for the multiply handicapped in suburban Chicago, maintains a living memorial plaque in its lobby. A gift of $50 will install the name of a departed loved one on the plaque. The school raised $9,000 from this source in a single year.

Some groups have profited by persuading their members to donate all of their trading stamps. The stamps are redeemed to provide gifts for door prizes and auction sales. One of the trading stamp companies has a special catalog that lists items available to organizations that collect huge quantities of stamps. It includes fire engines, ambulances, medical equipment, and playground and gymnasium equipment.

Many organizations in areas with public transportation have profited from the installation of benches at bus stops in busy locations. They sell advertising space on the benches to local business firms.

Using members' homes for receptions at which merchandise is sold, or services offered, can also be profitable. One group held a reception for a leading children's photographer who displayed his work. The organization received a commission on his sales to customers who were signed up at the reception.

19

Conclusion

This book was intended as a compendium of fund-raising events that would inspire the reader and aid in the selection of fund raisers appropriate for any size or type of organization. Once that selection has been made, the leadership of your organization should take advantage of other sources of information that will aid in conducting the event with maximum success.

Every type of event has its own characteristics—the do's and don'ts that determine success or failure. Before you get too deeply involved in the one you select, consult with others who have already sponsored similar events. They've gone through the learning curve and will be able to advise you on pitfalls you should avoid and opportunities you shouldn't miss. You will find most of them happy to share this information.

Consult your local library, or one of the regional libraries of the Foundation Center. Determine what books and pamphlets are available that describe, in detail, the kind of event that you have decided to sponsor.

Remember, always, that no event will realize its full potential without the enthusiastic support of all of your organization's members. Don't undertake one if there is dissension about the choice within the ranks. Your principal resource is people; trying to run a successful event with a halfhearted crew is like trying to win a harness race with a sick horse. You may reach the finish line but you won't win the purse.

Most important, follow all the guidelines offered in the first ten chapters and build a solid organization. Be especially mindful of fiscal management and the legal responsibilities of your group. If you do, your organization will thrive, and the cause you espouse will benefit from your efforts for many years to come.

Finally, don't let your fund-raising activities become a burdensome chore. Choose the ways of raising money that you and your members will enjoy.

In short, have fun!

Index

Videotape announcements, 38-
39
Voluntary agencies, 2
Volunteers, 4-5, 11, 16-18, 22, 75
recruitment, 5-6, 24-31
resources, 27-28, 76

W

Walking tours, 83
Washington, D.C.,
Metropolitan Police Boys
Clubs, 146
Wauconda (Ill.)
Transfiguration Parish, 93-
94
"Wedding, The," 136

Weight-A-Thon, 96
William Tell Pageant, 97
Wine and cheese parties, 126
Women's American
Organization for
Rehabilitation Through
Training (ORT), 81-82
Word-of-mouth, 41-42

Y

Yard work, 149

Z

Zoo-La-La, 119